SILVER
WHEN ALL IS LOST

by James R. Cook

Print and design by By All Means Graphics
Project management by Alecia Schreckenberg

ISBN: 978-1-7367891-1-7

TABLE OF CONTENTS

Introduction

INTRODUCTION

Whenever the left wins an election it propels us further along the road to a welfare state so expensive that it bankrupts the nation. Conservatives lose elections because the people on the dole turn out en masse to vote against them. They know that a liberal administration will lather out more benefits and subsidies without any concern for the economic consequences. Unfortunately, anything you subsidize, you get more of and that could serve as the nation's epitaph.

Now it seems possible that at some point in the future the U.S. will follow the Venezuelan example and vote for someone who promises to undo the Constitution and pass out money confiscated from the rich. America has taken a turn away from the principles that made us a great nation. It's sad to behold. The liberal agenda is the blueprint for national ruin and we are getting to see it in action.

From an economic standpoint, the left will cripple the economy with high taxes and inflate on a grand scale. Whenever you hear the word stimulus, replace it in your mind with the word inflating. Much of the money created by our central bank goes to pay for the social schemes that originated with the left. Expensive new programs are regularly introduced by progressives to give people free money. Liberals that run our central banks are going to pump up the stock market and monetize enormous quantities of debt. Consequently, the world could lose faith in the dollar. We never know what exactly lies ahead of us, but it's hard to be optimistic. The more you think about the left being in charge, the more you fear the probable outcome. The economic consequences of out-of-control spending, money creation and exploding government debt will at some point be devastating for the average American.

Recently, I was at a reunion lunch with my high school classmates. One of them asked me if I thought we had lived through a golden age? I said yes. Today, on top of our civic unrest, rising crime and our mutual antagonisms, we face the possible onset of runaway inflation followed by an economic collapse of epic proportions leading to a depression of unprecedented magnitude. The golden age has come and gone.

The reality is that we can't afford socialism, but we have it nevertheless. That makes national bankruptcy likely at some point in the future. As a consequence people should take measures to protect and preserve their financial well-being from the coming progressive onslaught. Silver serves that end and we advocate the ownership of physical silver coins and bars. This book makes the case that silver is one of the best things to own in a period when the radical left moves us towards economic ruin. In fact, having some silver on hand may, for a brief period of time, enable you to make transactions that keep you free of worry and stress.

CHAPTER ONE
INCOME INEQUALITY

"Conservatives are the primary producers within American culture. If we leave the leftists to their own devices there is a chance they will simply implode and eat each other because they have no idea how to fill the production void."

~Brandon Smith

"What's to stop bullying or harassment (much less looting, rioting and arson) when the media and Washington elite will consistently and helpfully write it off as just a bit of 'peaceful protest'?"

~Kimberly A. Strassel

"I am for doing good to the poor, but I differ in opinion of the means. I think the best way of doing good to the poor, is not making them easy in poverty, but leading or driving them out of it."

~Benjamin Franklin

It really gets tiresome listening to liberals complain about income inequality. Most of them know nothing about wealth creation or the incredible effectiveness of capitalism when it comes to delivering the goods. People get rich in America by providing goods or services that consumers prefer. New breakthroughs and innovations can make entrepreneurs wealthy. Microsoft made Bill Gates one of the richest persons to ever live. Has the accumulation of his great fortune hurt anyone? Who is suffering because of all the new millionaires and billionaires in the world? Did the poor get poorer? Of course not.

The left refuses to see that high incomes come from providing superior goods and services to consumers. Rockefeller made billions by providing oil for heating and lighting that was far cheaper than whale blubber. Henry Ford got rich making cars for the common man. The entrepreneurs that gave us the information age have been justly rewarded. Rich people are necessary and important. The countries with the highest standard of living have the most wealthy people. However, the left can't connect the dots. People get rich by growing a business and employing people. Wealthy people also create jobs through investments and through hiring people to provide services for them.

The so-called wealth gap is growing wider because more people are accumulating greater riches, not because more people are getting poorer. Yes, some people are stuck at the bottom, but not because of lack of opportunity. A poor person in America today is better off than most of the people that have ever lived.

Leftists never talk about the generosity and the enormous good that affluent people do with their fortunes. These charitable endeavors are enormously beneficial to mankind. Rich people give away a large percentage of their wealth to worthwhile causes – Carnegie's libraries, Gates in Africa. It's a perfect argument to counter the soak-the-rich schemes of the Democrats. Their high-tax policies destroy wealth and make everybody less well off. They see wealth as ill-gotten gain that must be redistributed. They see poverty rather than prosperity. They are a sorry lot of economic know-nothings who think they can replace capitalism with collectivism and make us better off.

The Democratic Party's dislike of capitalism has led them into a blind alley. By subsidizing people, the left is destroying their incentive to work and helped to make their incomes more unequal. Most people in America are doing pretty good these days. The shopping malls are full and new technologies keep us hopping. High incomes are a sign of prosperity and a successful economy. The best way to narrow income inequality is through a free enterprise system that gives everybody the opportunity to upgrade their earnings.

Every successful American with money should be alarmed at the current political bombast aimed at the rich. The left is ramping up hatred of capitalism and those who have acquired wealth. They are blaming free markets for poverty and economic hardship. They want the government to take away the assets of our most successful citizens. Throughout history hatred and dislike of those at the top has led to ruthless governments, revolutions and genocide. Numerous examples exist of misdeeds motivated by jealousy, intolerance or larceny. If you think that such things are impossible in America, history argues otherwise. The left preaches hatred, however subtle. Listen to the extremists among them and you will see the direction they are moving.

One of my neighbors is Armenian. His grandparents lived through the Armenian genocide that killed one-and-a-half million people. The Islamic Turks slaughtered the Christian Armenians. The Turks robbed, raped and murdered at will. My neighbor's grandmother came from a wealthy family and she and her sisters were raped and abused while everything they owned was stolen or confiscated. These gentle women were forced into a death march where thousands suffered and died. Why did these terrible atrocities occur? The Armenians were the most successful people in Turkey. They were often wealthy and they had accumulated more riches than the Turks. So they were envied and hated and ultimately murdered. The left stokes similar hatreds in America.

The media regularly reports left-wing accusations about the rich grabbing an unfair share. The goal is to sock it to the affluent with high taxes. We constantly read and hear about the far left economic theories of Krugman, Stiglitz, Piketty, Bernstein, Reich and the organizations that employ them. Most have views more in harmony with Marxists than free market economists. Almost everything that has been published on income inequality comes from left-wing think tanks and liberal organizations. None of it can be trusted.

Phil Gramm and John Early write, "The refrain is all too familiar: Widening income inequality is a fatal flaw in capitalism and an 'existential' threat to democracy. From 1967 to 2017, income inequality in the U.S. spiked 21.4%, and everyone from U.S. senators to the pope says it's an urgent problem. Yet the data upon which claims about income inequality are based are profoundly flawed.

"Census Bureau income data fail to count two-thirds of all government transfer payments – including Medicare, Medicaid, food stamps and some 100 other government transfer payments – as income to the recipients. Furthermore, census data fail to count taxes paid as income lost to the taxpayer. When official government data are used to correct these deficiencies – when income is defined the way people actually define it – 'income inequality' is reduced dramatically.

"We can now show that if you count all government transfers as income to the recipient household and reduce household income by taxes paid, not only is income inequality in America not growing, it is lower today than it was 50 years ago. The raging debate over income inequality in America calls to mind the old Will Rogers adage: 'It ain't what you don't know that gets you into trouble. It is what you do know that ain't so.' We are debating the alleged injustice of a supposedly growing social problem when that problem isn't growing, it's shrinking. Those who want to transform the greatest economic system in the history of the world ought to get their facts straight first."

You hear endlessly about the 1% who are getting richer. However, this is not at the expense of the 99% because the wealthy only make the economic pie bigger. If you change the world for the better, you deserve your billions. The income disparity that leftists rail about has a lot to do with social and cultural factors. The media reports that the rich are getting richer, but the poor are not joining in. That's because of problems like illegitimacy, addiction, educational shortcomings, criminality, one-parent families and the cult of victimhood. All of these pathologies are supported and encouraged by government subsidies. The high taxes that leftists argue for would make income inequality worse by keeping more people in poverty. If the left gets their way, we are all going to be poorer. Liberal economists without any business or practical experience advocate socialism and the media glorifies them. The educational system, the government and the media are in league to shove socialism down our throats. Our future hinges on the ability to thwart these redistributionists.

CHAPTER TWO
MEDIA PROPAGANDA

"In 1989, just two years before the Soviet Union collapsed, Paul Samuelson – the 'Father of Modern Day Economics' – and co-author William Nordhaus, wrote: 'The Soviet economy is proof that, contrary to what many skeptics had earlier believed, a socialist command economy can function and even thrive.'"

~M. N. Gordon

"Except for talk radio, liberals pretty much control the culture."

~Bernard Goldberg

"Capitalism needs neither propaganda nor apostles. Its achievements speak for themselves. Capitalism delivers the goods."

~Ludwig von Mises (1881-1973)

It's now to the point where you can't trust the reporting of the mainstream media. All along they have selectively reported the news. If it was negative for the left, they underreported or ignored it. Lately, I believe they have taken to reporting dishonestly. Our local newspaper has become one big editorial for left-wing causes. And they don't hesitate to stretch the truth or spread unfounded rumors. One of their biggest lies consists of stories about far-right groups who threaten disorder. They are trying to make right-wing extremists appear to be as numerous as the radical leftists, who are rioting frequently. The Minneapolis newspaper where I live often carries headlines about their evil intent, frequently referring to January 6th and exaggerating its effect. You couldn't have a better example of media distortions and dishonesty. Kimberly Strassel sums it up nicely in the Wall Street Journal, "Much of the press no longer has a commitment to truth, fairness or honesty. Its commitment is to Democratic power."

Most newspaper dailies in the U.S. are hopelessly liberal. The writers and editors have an unabiding hatred for capitalism, and the younger they are the worse it gets, it seems. They loathe free markets, the profit motive and rich white guys. Global warming gives newspapers a reason to tee off on the oil companies they hate. Their resistance to drilling and new pipelines borders on the irrational. In Minnesota a ragtag band of activists thwart a necessary pipeline and the newspaper features them as noble environmentalists. Day after day, the paper runs articles on weather extremes. They are clearly attempting to influence their readers to go all in on climate change. Editorials and opinions infect their news articles. They grossly violate the late newsman Jim Lehrer's rules of sound journalism, "Carefully separate opinion and analysis from straight news stories and clearly label everything."

Our nation's newspapers have sacrificed their integrity and objectiveness to become propaganda organs for the far left. In doing so, they have violated another of Jim Lehrer's rules, "Assume there is at least one other side or version to every story." The reason they are blind to the other side of the story is their hatred for free enterprise, business success and the merit system. Profits are a dirty word to them. Whether it be out of envy or runaway social sympathy these columnists, reporters and editorialists want to upend the system and make commerce conform to their concept of fairness, equality and social justice. They want high taxes, big government, hiring quotas, more business regulation and a free lunch. The future success of America depends on defeating them and their sorry redistributionist agenda.

Unfortunately, the liberal media is hastening the downfall of our country. They influence the thinking of the public. They glorify leftists like Ocasio-Cortez and make celebrities out of socialists. Critical Race Theory resonates with these liberal newsies. They constantly promote the left-wing agenda and try to persuade their audience of the validity of socialist causes. It's working. Their pernicious system is attracting adherents especially among the young. All of us underestimate the impact of years of liberal propaganda on the voters. They are turning the public against capitalism and free enterprise. They are constantly fomenting racial animosity, grudges and hatred. They are dusting off the failed Marxists' doctrines of class warfare, inequality and confiscatory taxation. They are the harbingers of decline and destitution. It can't get more serious for a country then to have collectivism on the rise.

It's not just the media, it's the educational system and the government itself that fosters the drumbeat of progressive propaganda. They are all doing public relations for the far left. This is how a great nation expires. When impressionable young people turn on the TV these days, they are overwhelmed with propaganda from the left. This daily bombardment in the media influences attitudes and voting decisions. The large number of young people who have changed their attitude towards big government and socialism is a consequence of the media's constant promotion of a left-wing agenda.

A federal judge recently said that the Democratic Party is close to controlling the press. He detailed what he described as shocking bias against Republicans. Circuit Court Judge Laurence Silberman outlined his opposition to the Supreme Court's key decision in 1964 in *New York Times v. Sullivan*, which has since protected many media outlets from lawsuits. Silberman wrote that the ruling is "a threat to American Democracy" and must be overturned. "The increased power of the press is so dangerous today because we are very close to one-party control of these institutions. Although the bias against the Republican Party is rather shocking today, this is not new; it is a long-term, secular trend going back at least to the '70s.

"Two of the three most influential papers, The New York Times and The Washington Post, are virtually Democratic Party broadsheets. And the news section of The Wall Street Journal leans in the same direction. The orientation of these three papers is followed by the Associated Press and most large papers (such as the Los Angeles Times, Miami Herald, and Boston Globe). Nearly all television – network and cable – is a Democratic Party trumpet. Even government-supported National Public Radio follows along."

Throughout my lifetime, the mainstream media have used television news as a means of persuasion. Liberal newsmen like Edward R. Murrow, Walter Cronkite, Chet Huntley, David Brinkley and Dan Rather were instrumental in selling the liberal agenda to the public. There's nothing subtle about it. They feed us radical liberal dogma that's somewhat remindful of a fanatical cult. For example, we've been bombarded with horror stories about climate change. When a liberal crackpot screamed that we would all be dead by 2020, the media made it sound like science. Most conservatives are unsure about global warming. They want sound evidence and they don't want to rush to judgment or take rash actions. The media brands them as "climate deniers" somehow akin to "Holocaust deniers." How fair is that? The left wants to override any opposing opinion and turn over the energy industry to the likes of AOC and Bernie.

What's most worrisome is that their media propaganda has worked. We are sliding further into government control and socialistic solutions for every problem. Endless amounts of money are funding income subsidies, unemployment benefits and new programs like daycare, free college and expanded medical coverage. The floodgates are open. If socialism wins, that will be the end of our freedom and prosperity. We will fail just as has every other country that fully adopted socialism.

Author David Horowitz explains how far left we have gone. "Today the ideological Left already controls a large swathe of the American present. It dominates the intellectual and popular cultures that shape its citizens' perceptions: the universities, the schools, the media, the entertainment industry, and the non-profit world of advocacy institutions which functions as a shadow political universe. Drawing on its prodigious power to affect the nation's consciousness, the Left – led by the New York Times and the Pulitzer Foundation – has systematically targeted the American Founding with the intention of burying the American idea and paving the way for a new anti-democratic order. America is unique among nations in being founded not on an identity rooted in 'blood and soil' but on a set of shared universal values. The American Founding in the revolutionary era 1776-1787 was based on what its creators regarded as 'self-evident' principles that provided the sinews of a national identity. Commitment to these principles has created a unity among the diverse peoples who have settled and occupied this country ever since. They have been the inspirational force enabling America to abolish slavery, become a universal symbol of freedom, and provide the world's chief bulwark against global tyrannies. It is this inspirational memory that the political Left has set out to erase and destroy."

The left in this country likes to link conservatives and libertarians to fascism. They utter warnings about what happened in Nazi Germany happening in America. They also advance the argument that the Nazis were right-wingers and foes of socialism. This, despite the fact the German fascists called themselves National Socialists. Conservative writers have often argued that the Nazis were socialists and had a kinship with the left more than the right.

In doing research for my website, neverforget.net, I recently read *Hitler – Memoirs of a Confidant*, a book about Otto Wagener. Hitler claimed Wagener was his closest confidant up until 1932. They parted ways because Wagener argued for a peaceful resolution with Russia and the other European countries. Wagener offers many quotes from Adolf Hitler including this: "It's true that I am a socialist."

CHAPTER THREE
WELFARE

"The welfare state is merely a method for transforming the market economy step by step into Socialism."
~Ludwig von Mises

"One of the consequences of such notions as entitlements is that people who have contributed nothing to society feel that society owes them something, apparently just for being nice enough to grace us with their presence."
~Thomas Sowell

"There are millions receiving government payments, who have come to consider them as an earned right, who of course find them inadequate, and who are outraged at the slightest suggestion of a critical re-examination of the subject. The political pressure for constant extension and increase of these benefits is almost irresistible."
~Henry Hazlitt (1894-1993)

Back in the 1930s when the government began to replace private charity with welfare programs, a stigma existed for those on the dole. Not all poor people signed up. Those who enrolled often had character issues. Even the earliest welfare rolls drew many people who saw it as a way out of work and responsibility. Yes, some had legitimate hardships, but many others were shirkers who made welfare a permanent lifestyle. The more they could get from the government, the less they had to adhere to the behavioral norms of the times.

Nothing enhances boredom like eliminating the requirement to make your own way in life. So almost from the beginning bored people who no longer had to work turned to mischief. This coarsening of behavior evolved into today's hideous social problems affecting welfare recipients including alcoholism, drug addiction, high crime rates, one-parent families and homelessness. This deterioration of the human condition has no parallel in history.

Unfortunately, the politicians and the government failed to see that their policies were hurting people more than helping them. Their social sympathy blinded them to the sorry results of permanently giving people money that they didn't earn. And so the accepted solution has been to give them more money through one government program after another. By every measure, they have become worse off and are continuing on this downward spiral.

Economist Justin Murray wrote, "During the 1960s the Great Society programs were implemented, particularly the War on Poverty. Over this period, spending on anti-poverty programs exploded five times in inflation-adjusted dollars, going from 3 percent of public spending to 20 percent between 1973 and today. Yet the poverty rate stubbornly ignored all this. None of these programs built in an incentive system to graduate people off of the assistance. These programs have generated a culture of dependency. The expansion of various handout programs (69 of them) has successfully eradicated the stigma of public assistance, removing the social pressure to improve. When nearly half the population receives public assistance, not including individuals receiving a paycheck for public sector work, people view it as normal and acceptable."

When I hear the socialist candidates for president claiming that "people are living from paycheck to paycheck," I think, so what? I've lived paycheck to paycheck including the first twenty years of marriage. Twice when I started businesses I went for months without any paycheck. At times in life you have to struggle and overcome financial difficulties. It's sickening how these leftists want to mollycoddle the citizenry. Grow up people. Do we have to run to the government with every hangnail?

When I was a young salesman, they opened an unemployment office in my town. One day I asked the office manager what they did. He told me they give money to people who are out of work. "Like who?" I wanted to know. He explained that construction workers who were laid off in the winter could get a monthly payment. This was a revelation to me and I wondered who would actually sign up for it. There was a heavy stigma against getting money from the government and nobody I knew would even consider it. How times have changed. Nobody thinks that way today. The rugged individualists of the past and our self-sufficient forebears never had a penny of subsidies. They made America great by overcoming difficulties and setbacks. They proved that people can get through anything on their own.

Alcoholism doesn't get enough blame in our discussions of poverty. Native Americans suffer an alcoholism rate as high as 90% on some reservations. Their social condition may be the worst in human history. Striking similarities exist between the reservations and the inner cities. The deterioration of the human condition is appalling in both places. Liberals insist that these deplorable conditions are the consequence of injustices perpetrated on these minorities. Their cure for this dysfunction is more subsidies even though giving people money doesn't appear to be improving their condition or lowering their affinity for alcohol and drugs. Whenever the welfare culture takes over in a neighborhood it goes to seed.

There is a tribe or ethnic population in Africa called the Igbo. They have suffered enormous persecution over the centuries from other Africans. Despite this adversity they are the wealthiest and most successful people in Africa. No population ever suffered the horrors and mass killings as did the Jews of Europe during the Holocaust. Yet out of this suffering came the modern nation of Israel. It's likely that Israel would not exist were it not for the Nazis. The few Jews who survived concentration camps have managed great success in both Israel and America after the war.

After the World War was over in the Pacific, the U.S. began to send monthly checks to islanders who may have been affected by the atomic bomb testing at Enewetak. These self-sufficient people were fishermen who lived successfully on the island. Soon they gave up fishing and relied on the government's monthly stipend. After a few decades, alcoholism became a raging problem and piles of empty beer cans dotted the island. These people are now, for the most part, helpless and unmotivated. The island is now known as "the slum of the Pacific." Nevertheless, nobody ever talks about examples like this when discussing the plight of the poor.

Wisconsin Senator Ron Johnson puts it this way, "President Lyndon

Johnson's Great Society programs were passed on the promise they would reduce poverty and strengthen the fabric of society. Although it is impossible to spend trillions and not do some good, data suggest these programs also did a great deal of harm. Before the Great Society, a booming economy was reducing poverty, and the national out-of-wedlock birthrate was only 4%.

"Fifty years later, 40% of all births occur outside marriage, deaths by suicide and drug overdose are rising, society is being torn apart by divisive forces, and many believe we need to spend trillions more to redress long-held grievances. It sure doesn't feel like we're better off. Rather than decreasing dependency, I would argue the Great Society increased it by weakening American families. Politicians of both parties whistle past this societal wreckage as they look for new excuses to spend even more money we don't have. They will celebrate their well-intentioned efforts and ignore the harmful consequences. What will those long-term consequences be? How will debt be paid? Most seem unwilling even to consider the question."

Lately I've been reading how the government won't be able to afford the retirement benefits and health care costs for retirees. I'll tell you what they are not going to be able to afford: a swelling population of the underclass who rarely work and live primarily off subsidies. In all too many cases these people have lost the ability to work. They're unemployable. Because they are bored, a lot of them make mischief and so we have a very expensive legal system with public defenders, court officers, judges, parole officers, wardens, police, guards and security personnel who would otherwise not be necessary. Then we have hospital emergency wards filled with victims of gunshot wounds, beatings and stabbings. In addition, there's the bad health of the underclass because of diet, booze and drugs. This drives up medical and health care costs for all of us.

James Howard Kunstler puts it this way, "In 2020, the half-century-long civil rights campaign that went up a dead end with all the family-destroying social services policies of the late 20th century, became such a manifestly embarrassing failure with an ever-growing hostile and dangerous underclass, that, in abject shame and disappointment, all of white liberaldom had to come up with an excuse for that failure, which finally fluoresced as Critical Race Theory with its hobgoblin-in-chief, systemic racism."

The government is also paying for a host of occupations that serve the bottom rung of society. Social workers have multiplied, as have chemical dependency counselors and job trainers. These all sound necessary, but never seem to help much. New prisons and hospitals, public transportation, patrol cars, homeless shelters and a million other expenses soak the government and the taxpayers. Social sympathy is running amok. These vast outlays add up to a scary number and there's a lot more to come. If we spend too much to make life easier, there will be consequences that make life harder. Empires have fallen and dynasties collapsed because they had a spending problem not unlike ours. Worst of all, the left will never stop spending (nor will many Republicans) and the dire consequences that follow (hyperinflation, depression) will play into the hands of the socialists. Once they get the upper hand, be assured that any semblance of the America you have known will disappear.

The underclass have helped turn Social Security into a partial welfare program. Anyone with a problem gets $1,200 a month. Filing a tax return brings another $1,200. Then there's various state welfare programs. There's the federal program that replaced Aid to Dependent Children. There's health care, food stamps, subsidized housing, rent and the payment of heating bills. Add to this the huge influx of illegal immigrants who require months and years of financial assistance. Some will be subsidized for the rest of their lives. If all these poverty programs were somehow reducing or curbing the population of the underclass, you could live with it. But, it's just the opposite. These subsidies attract people, and it's causing highly irresponsible parents to have offspring they don't take care of.

Author Mark Steyn points out, "Big Government's bias against marriage and family isn't an unforeseen quirk of the tax code. It's in logical, strategic support of its mission – to expand government and diminish everything else. How's it going? Well, 40 percent of American children are now born out of wedlock. A majority of Hispanic babies are born to unmarried mothers. So are 70 percent of black children. And so are 20 percent of the offspring of non-Hispanic white women with a high school education and an income under $20,000. Entire new categories of crime have arisen in the wake of familial collapse, like the legions of daughters abused by their mom's latest live-in boyfriend. Congressman Pence's doomsday scenario is already here: millions and millions of American children are raised in transient households and moral vacuums that make not just social mobility but even elemental character formation all but impossible. In an America of fewer jobs, more poverty, more crime, more drugs, more disease, and growing ethnocultural resentments, the shattering of the indispensable social building blocks will have catastrophic consequences."

These trends promise financial ruin and civil unrest. For one thing, taxes will be raised. Worst of all, the people paying the taxes are also paying to increase the threat to their safety and security from a growing horde of very bad actors. If the government ever fails to send out the welfare checks, nobody will be safe. Another way to put it is that we dare not reduce these payments for fear of riots and revolution. Once social welfare begins, it can't be stopped. That means welfare spending and the number of welfare recipients will likely increase over time. Looking into the future, the welfare problem could become so expensive it bankrupts the nation. So we are confronted with the Catch-22 of all time. How do we stop the growth of welfare before it proves fatal to the nation's finances and how do we do it without hurting people?

CHAPTER FOUR
INFLATION

"Nations are not ruined by one act of violence, but gradually and in an almost imperceptible manner by depreciation of their circulating currency, through its excessive quantity."
~Nicolaus Copernicus (1473-1543)

"The Fed will be proven catastrophically wrong about inflation for the simple reason that inflation isn't transitory, it's sticky: when prices rise due to real-world scarcities and higher costs, they stay high and then move higher as expectations catch up with reality."
~Charles Hugh Smith

"Inflation is a policy that cannot last."
~Ludwig von Mises

A discussion among economists of the Austrian school was recently printed in a publication of the Mises Institute in Auburn, Georgia. In commenting on warnings of inflation ahead economist Peter Klein said, "As the Austrians explained, a monetary-induced expansion is not indefinitely sustainable. You cannot create real wealth by turning on the money press. When will we see the effects play themselves out in terms of increases in prices? That's very difficult for us to say, and a lot of our enemies, the Krugmans of the world have been kind of beating Austrians over the head by saying, 'Oh, you guys have been predicting hyperinflation, but where is the hyperinflation? Obviously your theories are disproven by reality.'"

Lately, almost everyone can see serious inflation. In the past 10 years, inflating has been centered in assets. Stocks like GameStop, and cryptocurrencies like Bitcoin exemplify asset inflation. A painting by a computer that sells for $63 million and a LeBron James rookie bubble gum card that brings $5 million are outrageous examples of runaway asset inflation. The Bureau of Labor's inflation index of 2% doesn't harmonize with real-life experience. A visit to my dentist to pull a tooth and put in the foundation for an implant was $7,500. A friend recently got an estimate of $18,000 to fix his auto after a minor accident. When I first started in the precious metals business in 1973, an associate who worried about inflation made the shocking prediction that bread, which was then selling for $0.25 a loaf, would someday be $1.00 a loaf. We laughed at him.

If you own a lot of things, asset inflation can be quite enjoyable. However, when we begin to see price hikes in almost everything, it becomes painful for the citizenry. We are beginning to experience the painful variety of inflation as living costs go through the roof. The warnings of the Austrian school of economics are coming to fruition. The monetary authorities are flirting with disaster as they monetize the government's debt with newly created money.

Editor Michael Pento issued this warning, "The U.S. is mired in permanent QE, posting trillion-dollar deficits without end, and operating its government without a budget. We are sadly looking more like a banana republic every day. Two economists at the St. Louis Fed recently warned about the potential dangers involved when a nation's central bank buys its own debt. A solution some countries with high levels of unsustainable debt have tried is printing money. In this scenario, the government borrows money by issuing bonds and then orders the central bank to buy those bonds by creating (printing) money. History has taught us, however, that this type of policy leads to extremely high rates of inflation (hyperinflation) and often ends in economic ruin. This is exactly what the Fed has done and continues to do to this day. Not just a little bit but in a big way. The Fed has already permanently monetized nearly $4 trillion worth of debt and it is just getting started down this pernicious path. This strategy is a page taken from the how-to-be-a-banana-republic playbook and has been repackaged by some far-left politicians and pseudo-economists and renamed as Modern Monetary Theory. MMT is just a euphemism for debt monetization. Nevertheless, no matter what you call it, creating new money from nothing to purchase government debt has never worked in the history of economics and has always led to economic ruin."

With liberals in charge of our central bank and Treasury, the future of our currency and economy looks bleak. These are the same people who have made a mess of welfare, immigration, energy and education. The pied piper of Keynesian extremism, Paul Krugman of the New York Times advises the Fed and the administration not to worry about debt or inflation and to trust the government to fix the economy. Sad to say, once you've gone down this inflationary path for decades, there's no turning back unless you want to experience a depression. So the insanity of creating endless amounts of money until the currency implodes has become the liberal default position.

When you hear our monetary authorities actually endorse permanent levels of inflation, you know we are in trouble. No one has ever considered inflation to be a good policy until today. It's a liberal thing brought to you by the Keynesians at the Federal Reserve. The history of inflation through the ages offers a clear lesson that nations that inflate will eventually suffer grave consequences.

Author Charles Hugh Smith writes, "There's no failure that can't be glued together or covered up a bit longer with fountains of cash. That's the American way of solving problems, just throw more money at it. Health care is a leading example of this. The federal government's endless trillions boosted health care from 5% of the nation's economy to roughly 20% today. Health care is now so immense that it will bankrupt the nation all by itself.

"Also, look at what the Fed's endless monetary goosing has incentivized – a financial system addicted to 'free money,' soaring debt, accelerating leverage and near-infinite speculation. Given that the Fed has effectively promised to backstop all of Wall Street's bets, bail out every major player and never let the stock market falter for longer than three weeks, there is no risk at all in borrowing billions, leveraging it into tens of billions and then dumping these multiplying billions into the most speculative bets available. And so that's what every fund manager, hedge funder, punter, gambler and guru has done, and been richly rewarded for doing so.

"Sorry Fed, it's too late. The dominoes are already toppling, and every point of failure is being exploited. Every weak point – corruption, incompetence, bureaucratic sclerosis, regulatory thickets, and more of what's failed – will bring down existing systems with a momentum that will surprise all those who thought every system in America was rock-solid and forever."

The debasement of our money's purchasing power makes our living costs higher. In other words, inflation reduces our standard of living. That's one strike against it. We call it easy money, loose money, helicopter money or quantitative easing. It's responsible for low savings, excess debt, speculation, gambling, and overconsumption. That's two strikes against it. Inflation and socialism are joined at the hip. Newly created money pays the government's bills. It covers the welfare checks and the subsidies that have fostered dependency. Inflating has funded the stupendous breakdown of the family unit, encouraged illegitimacy, bad parenting and the coarsening of our culture. That's strike three.

Something I learned years ago struck a chord with me: "Money could never have originated as paper." This thought comes from the great Austrian school economist Ludwig von Mises, who said gold and silver evolved as money first and paper could only be money following these precious metals. In America, this process went through stages. First we had gold and silver coinage. Then we had gold- and silver-backed certificates which were similar to warehouse receipts. You could redeem your $20 bill (gold certificate) for $20 of actual gold. Redemption ended in America with Roosevelt in 1932 and for the world during the Nixon years.

So we've had fiat paper money for close to one hundred years. It's worked reasonably well. As a nation, we've prospered. The main worry about paper money is that there becomes too much of it. No brake exists on the creation of paper money. That enables the government to spend far more than they accrue through taxation. Now we appear to have lost control of the growth in money and credit. Central banks are printing money endlessly. This monetary excess has now spread throughout the world. It's Keynesian economics gone wild. The U.S. is considering following the Keynesian formula of withdrawing purchasing media during the boom. This has never been attempted before and if the Austrian school economists are right, stock and bond markets will crash and we will be back to printing money again.

It's hard to know if events are closing in on America, or if today's circumstances are the normal ups and downs of life on earth. When I was a kid in high school, we had the end of the Korean War, communists, atomic bombs, Russian spies and Joe McCarthy. My history teacher spent the entire semester denouncing Joe McCarthy. I didn't pay much attention to any of it.

Nowadays, the commies are back and the country has split into two bitter factions. Today, social issues and big government are the main themes that stoke hatred. All of this is probably not too different from past problems, but for one thing. This is the era in which we will get the verdict on the economic philosophy of John Maynard Keynes. As you know, Keynes advocated government intervention in the economy to rectify recessions or depressions. He argued that the government should create and spend large amounts of money to stimulate the economy in a slowdown. Then when things got heated, the government could withdraw the excess purchasing media it had previously created.

We may be at that juncture now. Can we stop quantitative easing (QE) and government programs that act as stimulus measures? The odds are against it. In fact, stopping QE could kill the economy. We have today's onerous levels of inflation because we've gone full-Keynesianism in this century. It looks like we are going to find it impossible to stop inflating. Keynes was a smart guy, but not smart enough to see that it would be impossible to repeal loose money policies without causing a crash.

Is this a bigger issue than what we've experienced in the past? Well it's not bigger than our wars. However, it's synonymous with our world dominance of the past 75 years and it can wreak havoc with our markets and our prosperity. It looks like the Keynesian formula won't work and runaway inflation is now entirely possible.

The ultimate outcome of the world's current monetary explosion (that cannot be terminated without a recession) is the destruction of paper money. That's where the world is heading – towards runaway inflation. Thus, it is a time to own tangible assets. Ultimately everything of paper will be decimated. For a hundred years we printed our way out of every economic contraction. That option now appears to be fraught with danger. The fact that so few see any problem should fortify the contrarians. Hedging against this dire outcome is imperative.

Analyst Daniel Oliver writes, "Hyperinflation generally occurs when the government forces its central bank to buy government bonds to fund persistent deficits even while the value of those bonds are collapsing. So it's not just that the quantity of notes is increasing but the collateral backing them is also rapidly becoming impaired.

"In these cases, there is no way for the central bank to intervene in the market to support its currency. The more it tries, in fact, by selling marketable assets to buy back its own currency, the worse the situation becomes because less collateral remains for the currency that remains outstanding – the same dynamic that drives a conventional bank run or the unwinding of an investment vehicle. This simple and obvious truth explains why central banks that find themselves defending their currency always fail: the market attacks them because their currencies are overvalued, and the more the bank sells its good collateral to buy back its own currency, the worse the situation becomes.

"There will come a time when money printing begins to lower, not increase, the total value of the dollar. At that point, the purchasing power of the state will begin to collapse even as the central bank is ordered to purchase more Treasuries. The U.S. will face a stark choice: follow the hyperinflationary path trod by so many other nations and empires or balance the federal budget."

CHAPTER FIVE

CANCEL CULTURE

"True advocates for diversity and inclusion should love no country on earth more than the United States. Our exceptional nation has taught the world that broad equality under the law provides a far better path to stability and prosperity than the perpetual struggle among divided groups ever could. That's why true opponents of racism oppose Critical Race Theory in our schools and elsewhere."
~Bruce Abramson

"It is clear that the political left has gone so far off the rails into its own cultism that there is no coming back."
~Brandon Smith

"California is at it again, editing language to alter reality. San Francisco just changed 'felon' to 'justice involved person.'"
~Simon Black

"In America, you disrespect the institutions of your country, and you get lionized by the media. You take a knee or turn away from the flag or refuse to take the field or the court while the national anthem is played, and you get nodding assent from the authorities who control the sport."
~Gerard Baker

When I'm in Florida for the winter, I subscribe to the Sarasota Herald-Tribune. When reading the paper I always check a cartoon called Mallard Fillmore that pokes fun at progressives. Wouldn't you know it, they canceled Mallard Fillmore. They put a notice in the cartoon section and when I read it, I became angry enough to send the paper an email that I was canceling my subscription. I noticed a couple of letters on the editorial page also complaining about the loss of Mallard and promising an end to their home delivery.

Do the leftists promulgating this cancel culture think that somehow these actions are going to eliminate racism? Liberals think they have the moral high ground because they've convinced themselves that 150 million people on the right are racist. They feel justified in doing anything they wish to punish conservatives and banish their supposed prejudices. The most militant among them are now condemning our founding fathers and even attempting to censor what we read.

The hard left claims everyone with light skin is a racist. Nothing could be further from the truth. Most conservatives are happy to see successful minority persons and bear no ill will towards anyone striving to get ahead in life. When we condemn riots, looting, crimes and misbehavior, it's not racism, it's common sense. When you hear these left-wing agitators condemning law enforcement, abolishing police protection and weakening law and order, it sounds crazy to us. We want the best for all races and we know that this kind of radical agenda won't get it done.

Author Judith Bergman writes, "A recent survey of 2,000 Americans by the Cato Institute found that 62% of Americans say 'the political climate these days prevents them from saying things they believe because others might find them offensive... Nearly a third (32%) of employed Americans say they are worried about missing out on career opportunities or losing their job if their political opinions became known.'

"The survey also found that younger Americans under 30 were more concerned than older Americans that their political opinions could harm their careers. That young people especially are afraid to speak their minds – the survey suggests this is because they 'have spent more time in America's universities' – is particularly worrying. American campuses have steered a 'leftist' course for decades. The tilt has had familiar consequences: the proliferation on campus of 'safe spaces,' trigger warnings, de-platforming of conservative voices and a 'cancel culture' aimed at professors and students who do not conform to an on-campus political orthodoxy that has become increasingly totalitarian. Most recently, the dean of the University of Massachusetts-Lowell's School of Nursing, Leslie Neal-Boylan, was fired by the school after writing 'everyone's life matters' in an email to students and faculty.

"Cancel culture has moved from campus into American society. The topics no longer seen as legitimate subjects of free and open public debate keep growing: Race, gender, the merits of Western history and civilization, and climate change currently top the list of taboo subjects. In addition, there are words and concepts that are no longer considered legitimate. Those who publicly offer dissenting views on any of these issues risk immediate 'cancellation.' The chilling effects that these 'cancellations' have on people are severe and should not be underestimated.

"The free exchange of opinions and ideas is the bedrock of healthy democracies. How much speech can you shut down – and how many people can you 'cancel' – before public discourse is destroyed altogether? A democratic society of fearful citizens who dare not speak about what is on their minds is doomed to succumb to the will of those who bully the hardest and shout the loudest."

If the lunatics on the left ever get the upper hand you can say goodbye to the America we know and love. Liberals have veered so far off the tracks you wonder about their sanity. The Democratic Party is gripped by crazy ideas and a fanaticism that borders on madness. Their ideas are the blueprint for the disintegration of our society. This is the greatest threat our nation has ever faced. Make no mistake, a victorious left can eventually lead to our destruction. Liberals want to tamper with the Constitution and the checks and balances our forefathers established. They hope to pack the Supreme Court with additional progressive judges. They want to kill the Electoral College. They want to abolish the Second Amendment and eventually eliminate gun ownership. They intend to allow felons to vote and they want to reduce the voting age.

The left wants open borders that allow any and all to enter the country with full access to welfare. They advocate sanctuary cities where criminals who are in the country illegally are protected and nurtured. They want to eliminate the agency that enforces our immigration laws. They refuse to acknowledge any type of problem with the flow of immigrants at our border and they resist a wall that would reduce the heavy drug smuggling into our country. They want to increase welfare payments and give more money to social programs. They want to give a lump sum payment to anyone who can trace their ancestry back to slaves that lived 150 to 300 years ago. They want to increase taxes to draconian levels including an annual wealth tax on every asset. They want a guaranteed income for every shirker and free college and free health care for all.

Peggy Noonan writes in the Wall Street Journal, "The past decade saw the rise of the woke progressives who dictate what words can be said and ideas held, thus poisoning and paralyzing American humor, drama, entertainment, culture and journalism. In the coming 10 years someone will effectively stand up to them. They are the most hated people in America, and their entire program is accusation: you are racist, sexist, homophobic, transphobic; you are a bigot, a villain, a white male, a patriarchal misogynist, your day is over. They never have a second move. Bow to them, as most do, and they'll accuse you even more of newly imagined sins. They claim to be vulnerable victims, and moral. Actually they're not. They're mean and seek to kill, and like all bullies are cowards. Everyone with an honest mind hates them. Someone will finally move effectively against them. Who? How? That will be a story of the '20s, and a good one."

If we lose to "the woke," the cancel culture will abridge our right to free speech and punish those who dare speak out. The merit system will be subject to bitter attack and quota systems will be enforced by law. An aggressive confiscation of firearms will render the Second Amendment irrelevant. Taxes on incomes and assets will rise to confiscatory levels. The oil and gas industry will be regulated out of business and perhaps nationalized. Crimes will be overlooked and punishment reduced. Capitalism will be demeaned and overregulated. Socialist schemes will eliminate profits and sink the economy.

Author Victor David Hanson writes, "Name one mainline institution that the woke left does not now control – and warp. The media? The campus? Silicon Valley? Professional sports? The corporate boardroom? Foundations? The K-12 educational establishment? The military hierarchy? The government deep state? The FBI's top echelon? This time around, members of the left really believe that 'by any means necessary' is no mere slogan. Instead, it is a model of how to disrupt or destroy American customs, traditions and values.

"Woke revolutionaries are not panhandlers, street people or Grateful Dead groupies. They are not even a few nutty and murderous Symbionese Liberation Army terrorists fighting against 'the Man.' They are top-down revolutionaries. None of their agendas, from open borders and changing the Constitution to critical race theory and banning clean-burning fossil fuels, are ever favored among a majority of the population. Their guiding principle is 'never let a crisis go to waste.' Only in times of a pandemic, a national quarantine or volatile racial relations can the new upscale leftist revolutionaries use fear to push through policies that no one in calm times could stomach.

"Our revolutionaries hate dissent. They destroy any who question their media-spun hoaxes. Truth is their enemy, and fear is their weapon. Sixties paranoid revolutionaries warned about George Orwell's '1984,' but our revolutionaries are '1984.' While this elitist leftist revolution is more dangerous than its sloppy '60s predecessor, it is also more vulnerable, given its obnoxious, top-heavy apparatus – but only if the proverbial 'people' finally say to their madness, 'Enough is enough.'"

Editor Mike Adams writes, "Lunatic left-wing Democrats are now flatly incompatible with civil society. They cannot function in a system rooted in fairness, free speech and equal protection under the law. They can only flourish under rigged, authoritarian systems, rooted in government tyranny and the destruction of fundamental human rights such as the right to speak. Democrats have been transformed into hate-filled, raging lunatics who cannot function under a system of law or reason."

Wall Street Journal editor Daniel Henninger agrees: "Conclusive evidence has emerged that the American left is certifiably insane. After the shooting of two cops in Compton, south of Los Angeles, a small contingent of antipolice protesters stood outside a hospital chanting, 'We hope they die!' We don't make the left-is-insane charge lightly. It is common practice for these protesters, men and women, to stand inches from the faces of cops, especially black cops, screaming insults and personal obscenities with no letup. This behavior is a phenomenon worth thinking about. So my argument: The Democratic left has turned certifiably insane."

Nevertheless, the cancel culture is riding high. For example, the Yale Daily News writes, "Yale will stop teaching a storied introductory survey course in art history, citing the impossibility of adequately covering the entire field – and its varied cultural backgrounds – in one course. This change is the latest response to student uneasiness over an idealized Western 'canon' – a product of an overwhelmingly white, straight, European and male cadre of artists." So that's it, apparently: the great masterpieces recognized as such by the entire world for generations are now tainted by their supposed "whiteness" and must be censored.

Here's more of the same: "Bloomberg reports the era of the white, all-male board is coming to an end. Goldman Sachs Group Inc. Chief Executive Officer David Solomon issued the latest ultimatum. Wall Street's biggest underwriter of initial public offerings in the U.S. will no longer take a company public in the U.S. and Europe if it lacks a director who is either female or diverse. The mandate is the latest in a series of signals that non-diverse boards and management are unacceptable. Public companies with all-male boards based in California now face a $100,000 fine under a new state law. Fred Foulkes, a management professor at the Boston University Questrom School of Business said, 'If the board has all white males, that's a big negative.' Next year, the bank will raise the threshold to two diverse directors, which includes diversity based on sexual orientation and gender identity."

Editor Brandon Smith warns, "The social justice cult never sleeps, they are forever 'woke.' The mainstream media constantly mentions 'white supremacists,' 'neo-Nazis' and 'extremists' within the same articles they mention 'conservatives.' Though there is no evidence whatsoever to link the majority of conservatives with race identity groups, the hope within the establishment is that the conservative base in the U.S. can be dismantled through guilt by manufactured association."

How does America stack up against the evils of other major countries over the past hundred years? Let's consider Russia. They murdered 25 million of their own people. How about China? The Marxists killed 65 million of their own citizens. What about Japan? Estimates of death perpetrated by the Japanese in World War II run as high as 10 million.

Let's not forget Germany. The Germans slaughtered up to 30 million innocents including Russians, Poles, Jews, Gypsies and other Europeans. Many of these killings were accompanied by brutal torture and unprecedented savagery.

How does that compare with the so-called sins of the U.S.? America went to war to put an end to many of these killings. We built a great economic superpower that lifted much of the world's population from poverty, disease and starvation. We dramatically improved the living standards of our citizens and provided them with abundance. We have been the greatest force for good and common sense in the history of our planet. We have blessed the earth with our kindness and decency. We are anything but evil.

When it comes to politics, the trend is not our friend. The woke have made too many inroads in recent years. When have there ever been radical leftists with enough clout to cancel aspects of our culture? Never before have socialists like Ocasio-Cortez and the Squad become media darlings. Their overwrought hatred of free enterprise, capitalism and the merit system should send a chill up the spine of every successful or rational person.

They would not hesitate to change the Constitution to meet their policy goals. They have allies in the schools and colleges who are undermining the reputation of our founding fathers and their legacy of freedom. They claim that slavery built America never mentioning that America blossomed after it ended slavery. The industrial revolution occurred after the civil war was over. They twist American history into a tale of exploitation and injustice. They write off those who have succeeded in our country as a privileged minority undeserving of their affluence.

They are the stepchildren of Marx and Lenin promoted by fellow travelers in the media and useful idiots in the liberal wing of their party. I cannot stress enough how dangerous these comrades are to the way of life we have enjoyed for a hundred years. There are elements among them who would not hesitate to employ violence in the expropriation of private assets should the opportunity arise. The leftist hero of the Cuban revolution, Che Guevara, would simply murder the rich landowners who balked at turning over their land. We all know of the horrors perpetrated by Stalin to further his goals. Socialism cannot erase the atrocities, killing and brutality that inevitably accompany its rise to political control of a nation. The fact that so many in the media, the government and the schools have influenced young people to favor its enactment should strike anxiety in the heart of every citizen.

Author James Howard Kunstler makes this prediction, "In the new year, the ongoing economic carnage will be so severe that the nation may not have time for the finer points of Woke theory and philosophy. Woke cries of "racist, racist, racist" will no longer be greeted with supplication, apologies, and cosseting. For the first time in decades in the USA, everyone will have to pull his or her own weight, and shut the **** up about it. Hard times will shake America out of its squishy fantasies and concentrate millions of minds on looking after their basic needs without mommy-hugs or affirmative action line-jumping.

"Antifa, a Woke auxiliary with a really bad attitude, spent most of the Covid-19 year in Seattle, Portland, Minneapolis, Philly, and NYC where feckless politicians forced police to stand down, or crippled them with sanctions against the use of force. Antifa rioters discovered that it was especially fun to play adult versions of capture-the-flag on warm summer nights with the cops. They got to wear groovy street-fighting outfits and wield umbrellas against gas attacks, and the hormonal young men showboated acts of derring-do with fireworks, skateboards, baseball bats, and, more than once, alas, firearms. If they happened to get rounded up by the police, the local DAs let them go and many returned to the fun riots time after time, all summer long.

"A lot of property got damaged, statues of famous Americans got pulled down, spray-painted, peed-on, busted up, decapitated. Businesses having a hard enough time staying afloat under the Covid-19 lockdowns, had their storefronts smashed, equipment and merchandise looted. Fifty years from now, wrinkled old Antifas will recall how romantic it was. Soon, the public will lose patience with any further Antifa antics in the streets. They will get their umbrellas shredded and their asses kicked, and they'll go weee-weee-weee back to mommy's basement."

Author Brandon Smith explains, "I've been writing about political correctness and woke culture for a long time now, and I have to say that the developing trends of social justice are not surprising. However, the speed at which they are being forced on the rest of us today is disturbing. One has to wonder if the woke mob is in a rush to meet some kind of propaganda deadline the rest of us are not aware of.

"The gender and 'trans' issues are really at the forefront of leftist ideology these days. You are probably aware that people who claim to be trans earn an automatic spot at the top of that totem pole, well above women, black people, and even your run-of-the-mill gay people. The trans costume is most powerful and imbues a person with unlimited protection no matter how terrible that person might be. It even allows them to dictate the very thoughts and speech of the public at large.

"It is important to note that the trans identity is a sort of magic ticket for white people in particular. The Social Justice Warrior (SJW) cult is especially concerned with all white people (mainly white men) as some kind of monstrous threat to the safety and emotional stability of everyone else. If you are a white person within the SJW religion you are immediately hated for your original sin and are relegated to the leftist gutter. They despise your skin color, and no amount of help you give as an 'ally' is going to earn you a place among the oh-so-holy oppressed.

"Unless, that is, you say you are trans. Then, as if you have touched the pure hand of the SJW deity, you are suddenly absolved of all your inherent white evil and are given a mantle of divinity. You are better than everyone else, because you are supposedly the most oppressed of them all.

"Maybe this sounds like a bit of exaggeration. Surely I am engaging in hyperbole. I promise you I am not. Western culture is being increasingly segregated by the political left into various tiers of people based on their skin color as well as their sexual orientations and mental instabilities, and the more made-up the orientations and the more volatile the mental instability the more privileges a person is afforded. The patients are truly taking over the asylum."

CHAPTER SIX
WELFARE WORRIES

"Progressives can win elections, but there's a problem: They don't know how to govern."
~Daniel Henninger

"Never underestimate the power of envy and a desire of some to get something for nothing. Feeding that desire with state power leads to dependence, entitlement, resentment and an unquenchable thirst for more."
~Gary Daniels

"The only way to break the cycle of unwed motherhood, fatherless children, poverty, crime and welfare is to recognize that welfare causes more problems than it cures."
~David Boaz

Since the administration of Franklin Roosevelt the government has tried to improve the condition of the poor. In terms of material things like cell phones and TVs their lot in life has improved. The same can't be said about their behavior, which has deteriorated. The more the poor of all races were helped and subsidized, the more dysfunctional they became. The trillions spent to ameliorate poverty has brought instead a plague of alcoholism, drug addiction, crime, homelessness, abuse, bad parenting, delinquency and character issues that inhibit employment. All this was accompanied by an attitude of entitlement among welfare recipients that has morphed into a festering resentment that blames others for their predicament.

A rational society blames the sinner. However, what has evolved on the left is to blame successful people for the plight of the underclass. The call for social justice resonates in the media, the educational system and the government. At the heart of it is the belief in redistribution. Take the money from those who earned it and give it to those who didn't. While you're at it, reduce the penalties for crimes and overlook bad behavior. Despite this national emphasis on social justice and redistribution, the misbehavior of the subsidized is getting worse. It has deteriorated through eight decades of social welfare and it will be much worse in the future. Virtually everything the left stands for promotes the destruction of civil society.

Writing in the Wall Street Journal, Daniel Henninger agrees: "A claim made repeatedly this week is that the American people, are guilty of perpetual 'systemic racism.' Great Society programs that have been in place 55 years totaling trillions of dollars on Medicaid, food stamps, welfare, public housing, rent subsidies and federal aid to public schools have produced . . . what?

"Since the 1960s, essentially little has changed in the neighborhoods at the center of those long-ago urban riots. By current telling, they are about as poor, as crime-ridden, as under-educated and in poor health as they were when LBJ said he would change them. That means five decades of stagnation in America's most marginalized places, virtually all of it under Democratic – now 'progressive' – political control. The failure of the liberal model is by now so embarrassing that the current owners of that model have created an alternative universe of explanations, [including] systemic racism."

When a big city elects a liberal mayor, you can be sure practical solutions to problems will be jeopardized. In St. Paul, Minnesota an outbreak of shooting and killing on city streets has alarmed the citizenry. The police want to install something called a ShotSpotter which immediately notifies them where a shot was fired. This has been effective in other cities to reduce shootings. The police also want to add more officers.

The mayor wants none of this. He advocates community ambassadors, government outreach and encouraging landlords to rent to felons. He wants an extra million and a half for a more "holistic" approach to crime. This is the standard liberal prescription; more money and more social programs. These solutions never seem to work. Crime grows more persistent. Meanwhile, the police must now ignore traffic violations and shoplifting. In California, programs are underway to pay criminals for not shooting anyone.

The young shooters and gang members responsible for these killings aren't going to stop because of government money. They got this way because of the horrible way too many were brought up. If your parents are criminals or addicts, you're likely to be of equally low character. There is only one solution and it's not popular. Take these abused and neglected infants away from toxic parents. In the right homes these children will be graduating from college instead of going to prison.

At one time orphanages like Father Flanagan's School in Nebraska were accepted by society. For the most part, these kids turned out to be law-abiding citizens. A good-hearted woman tried to open such a facility in Minnesota a few years ago and the media and minorities tore her apart. So that's a solution that won't be tried. The shooters will keep shooting and liberals will be wrong about this as they are about almost everything.

Analyst Steve Feinstein writes, "Many major U.S. cities run by liberal Democrats are in rough shape. They are afflicted by the problems of homelessness, violent crime, gangs, and unemployment to a far greater degree than the country as a whole. As Investor's Business Daily put it: 'When Democrats are in control, cities tend to go soft on crime, reward cronies with public funds, establish hostile business environments, heavily tax the most productive citizens and set up fat pensions for their union friends.'

"Liberal governing practices of wealth redistribution, punitive taxation, and excessive regulations all combine to produce the unintended consequence of short-circuiting personal initiative and ambition. Instead, these excessive giveaway programs essentially 'teach' people how to game the system and get the government to pay for their existence in society. Liberal cities are governed by the guiding tenets of softness, misplaced 'compassion,' and individual unaccountability.

"Liberal policies have worked almost perfectly to degrade the quality of inner-city life for their residents. Instead of raising the standard of living for all the city's inhabitants, excessive giveaways and lax or missing enforcement of local laws have the opposite effect. Such governmental practice only teaches people that they are forever unaccountable as regards the norms of society and that they will be given their daily sustenance for free, without putting forth any commensurate effort on their part."

Years ago a well-known Democrat wrote that every time a person gets mugged the Democrats lose a vote. In other words the victim of a car-jacking no longer has much social sympathy. Experiencing such a crime changes them forever. How about the crimes and rioting in our major liberal cities, will that change voter sentiments? It would seem that these looters and shooters are playing into Republican hands. If a majority of the American people do not deplore these riots and begin to reflect these sentiments at the ballot box, it would be a sure sign of national decay.

Unfortunately, the view that looting acts as a form of reparations has gained a following among the more militant racial grievance groups. Furthermore, the rioters and looters have essentially gone unpunished for their misdeeds. Actually, they were rewarded with luxury goods, liquor, TVs and electronic devices. All of this acts as an incentive for more looting. When a minority person recently committed suicide in downtown Minneapolis, social media mistakenly reported it as a police shooting. Within minutes rioters smashed their way into a Target store and began stealing the inventory. From there rioting spread through downtown.

In other words, this new trend of criminality may be far from over. This is especially true if the police continue to be onlookers and the politicians appear to condone these outbreaks. How bad will it get? It could be enough to keep people out of large parts of major cities and that would hurt merchants and property owners. Riots also act to unnerve and unsettle the population. Thus the economy suffers. Radicals are plotting right now to wreak havoc. Make sure you're not in their way. These people are a risk to everything you hold dear.

Ryan McMaken writes, "It's now become fashionable on the left to defend looting as a means of redistributing wealth. In a new book titled *In Defense of Looting*, Vicky Osterweil identifies herself as 'a writer, editor, and agitator based in Philadelphia.' Osterweil states: 'When I use the word looting, I mean the mass expropriation of property, mass shoplifting during a moment of upheaval or riot. It tends to be an attack on a business, a commercial space, maybe a government building – taking things and sharing them for free.' Osterweil then goes on to assert that looting is basically a poverty relief program, and it liberates the looters from having to work for a living: 'It gets people what they need for free immediately, which means that they are capable of living their lives without having to rely on jobs or a wage.'

"If only there were more looting, we could all 'have things for free': '[Looting] attacks the idea of property, and it attacks the idea that in order for someone to have a roof over their head or have a meal ticket, they have to work for a boss, in order to buy things that people just like them somewhere else in the world had to make under the same conditions. It points to the way in which that's unjust. And the reason that the world is organized that way, obviously, is for the profit of the people who own the stores and the factories. So you get to the heart of that property relation, and demonstrate that without police and without state oppression, we can have things for free.'"

What kind of crazy communist thinking is that? What really happens if the welfare checks stop coming? The constant inflating of money and credit to pay for runaway government welfare spending can't go on forever. Then, you have the possibility of hyperinflation or the depreciation of the dollar in foreign exchange markets. At some point the government may not be able to borrow what they need while tax revenues fall off precipitously. It's possible the time will come when the money isn't there to pay the bills. It may sound far-fetched today, but present spending trends make such a financial crisis inevitable.

How will the underclass react if they don't get their welfare checks? Radical leftists would likely win the vote. New taxes would confiscate most of the wealth. The rich would be squeezed and berated. Government would nationalize industries and enforce mindless regulation. Crime would reach epidemic proportions with robberies and burglaries terrifying city neighborhoods. Police would be overwhelmed with riots and demonstrations. The spending cutbacks would plunge the economy into a recession and depression. Some sort of nightmare scenario is inescapable if current spending and inflating continue unchecked. Unfortunately, stopping these policies threatens an equally bad outcome. We are truly between a rock and a hard place. We will continue to kick the can down the road until there's no road left. The final reckoning won't be pretty.

Liberals justify law-breaking and vandalism as the result of racial grievances. They stress that today's demonstrations are mostly peaceful. After seeing the burned-out hulks of once vibrant businesses it should be hard for voters to swallow this malarkey. When the police don't come for a 911 call that means your personal safety is at risk. Hopefully most people don't have to get mugged before they see the light.

The author Abigail Shrier writes about these criminal acts, "The frequency of assaults in the New York area targeting ultra-Orthodox Jews is alarming. Videos of the Brooklyn assaults seem borrowed from another time and place: of Jews attempting to mind their own business in black hats and dark suits beaten by street thugs.

"Our sin was to have whitewashed the Crown Heights pogrom of 1991 and lavished its instigator Al Sharpton with respectability. After a car crash involving a Hasidic driver resulted in the death of Gavin Cato, the 7-year-old son of Guyanese immigrants, Mr. Sharpton led a three-day riot in Crown Heights. He blamed the accident on "diamond merchants," and his followers chanted, "Kill the Jew." They did. The Jew they killed was Yankel Rosenbaum, 29, a doctoral candidate from Australia. Nearly 200 more were injured in the melee. The political and media elites forgave Mr. Sharpton. Democrats called no harm, no foul. The ultra-Orthodox vote Republican anyway. Mr. Sharpton rose to the Democratic debate stage in 2004 and now hosts a show on MSNBC. This year's Democratic candidates for president have kissed his ring. And so the ultra-Orthodox Jews find themselves sitting ducks again in a New York hostile or indifferent to their fate.

"There is a moral imperative. Because an America that allows its religious minorities to be harassed, assaulted and murdered in the streets is not a free country at all. If religious liberty means anything today, then it must be something we afford those peaceful minorities whose political views have become unfashionable, whose customs appear to be throwbacks, who remind us more of another place and time, where they were hunted and killed in unspeakable numbers. At stake isn't merely the lives of these Jews, but the soul of a nation that once welcomed and embraced them."

Author Erico Matias Tavares defends America against the accusation of racism. "No country is perfect and all have difficult pasts. America is no different here. But having lived all over the world, in many different countries and cultures, I can unequivocally state that America is the least racist and most open today. Why would anyone move their family to a country where they will be 'systemically oppressed' by 'white supremacists'? This makes no sense of course. Because it is not true.

"Police in America do not go around killing black people. In 2019, nine unarmed blacks were shot and killed by cops in a country of 320 million, compared with fifteen whites. Nine is too many at first blush, but certainly does not justify dumping the Constitution, looting and burning cities to the ground. I'm aware of the difficulties faced by black people in the U.S., having closely interacted with many over the years. The narrative is that this is caused by white racism. Perhaps this is true in some instances – managing a multi-ethnic society is not easy. However, growing up in a home without a father plays a far more deleterious role: 75% of black children today live with a single parent. That is a horrific statistic that should get far more publicity.

"The real culprit here is an incompetent and corrupt governing class who with their media minions constantly agitate for racial division – including pushing hatred and demonization of cops and whites in general. America, which is not my country, has given me a career, a corporate education, timeless entertainment, friends, a home where people of all races interact with and smile at each other in the street, and most important of all – my family. It was because of the countless sacrifices of Americans that I was able to grow up in a part of the world free from communism, fascism and oppression. The monuments that remind us of their bravery should be revered, not defaced or taken down. Americans of all colors are good people. We should build upon the many good things that have been achieved with tremendous difficulty over centuries and make them better – an example that other countries can follow. If America fails, the world will be a far worse place as a result. Of that much we can all be certain."

CHAPTER SEVEN
COMMIES

"For a generation after the fall of the Berlin Wall in 1989, most Americans and Europeans regarded Marxism as an enemy that had been defeated once and for all. But they were wrong. A mere 30 years later, Marxism is back, and making an astonishingly successful bid to seize control of the most important American media companies, universities and schools, major corporations and philanthropic organizations, and even the courts, the government bureaucracy, and some churches."
~Yoram Hazony

"An entire generation of American adults is too young to remember the suffering socialism caused during the 20th century. Collective historical ignorance is becoming a real threat. Those of us who remember have a responsibility to educate young Americans about the poverty and tyranny that inevitably follows socialism."
~Nikki Haley

"Salvation by society failed the most where it promised the most, in the communist countries. But, it also failed in the west. Practically no government program enacted since the 1950s in the Western world has been successful."
~Peter Drucker (1909-2005)

If you had any doubts about the warped perceptions of the left, recent political warfare should put that to rest. Today's liberals make things up to suit their political purpose. They see things through a filter of radical leftism where the means are justified by the end. They would not hesitate to overturn the Constitution for their favorite social schemes. They sometimes shut down their opponents with storm-trooper tactics that we see employed by Antifa and campus radicals. They are so certain of their moral superiority and the truthfulness of their liberal dogma they will do the nasty things in America that collectivists have always done to gain power. Ultimately, they will try to take everything you have and they will brutalize you if you resist. Don't think for a moment that progressives are not the greatest enemy the American way of life has ever faced. Their mandate for social justice and social change will preempt your freedom in a heartbeat.

Worst of all they are evolving further leftward; from democrat to liberal to socialist to collectivist. The ugly history of Castro and Stalin does not register with them. They just keep marching towards the hell on earth that is state control. The liberals don't even know what they are walking into but the Marxist radicals certainly know. These collectivists hate America. They claim our country was never exceptional. And who is to blame for all the injustice those socialists see? Who is responsible for causing people to be poor and homeless? Well it's simple, the American people are.

Author Mark Levin writes, "In America, many Marxists cloak themselves in phrases like 'progressives,' 'Democratic Socialists,' 'social activists,' 'community activists,' etc., as most Americans remain openly hostile to the name Marxism. They operate under myriad newly minted organizational or identifying nomenclatures, such as 'Black Lives Matter' (BLM), 'Antifa,' 'The Squad,' etc. And they claim to promote 'economic justice,' 'environmental justice,' 'radical equality,' 'gender equity,' etc. They have invented new theories, like Critical Race Theory, and phrases and terminologies, linked to or fit into a Marxist construct. Moreover, they claim "the dominant culture" and capitalist system are unjust and inequitable, racist and sexist, colonialist and imperialist, materialistic and destructive of the environment. Of course, the purpose is to tear down and tear apart the nation for a thousand reasons and in a thousand ways, thereby dispiriting and demoralizing the public; undermining the citizenry's confidence in the nations institutions, traditions, and customs; creating one calamity after another; weakening the nation from within; and ultimately, destroying what we know as American republicanism and capitalism."

The Russian revolutionary V.I. Lenin thought that a dedicated cadre of Marxist revolutionaries could lead people into overthrowing the existing order. He was right. When I hear Marxists at our universities expressing hatred for America and denouncing us for our crimes in various parts of the world, it sounds like they have a revolution in mind. At such times, it's good to remember that the Marxists were responsible for the murder of 100 million people and in that respect were worse than the Nazis.

Marxist radicals want to trash capitalism and eliminate the market economy. They want to generate class warfare and turn the people against one another. Ultimately, they wish to expropriate wealth and redistribute it into their own hands much as did the Bolsheviks in Russia. The Reds would round up the farm families who opposed their confiscation of land and crops and load them on trains to Siberia where they were pushed out in the dead of winter with no shelter. These Marxist revolutionaries found grisly ways to torture and kill anyone who opposed them.

It's truly amazing that this horrible collectivist doctrine still has people promoting it. They teach it at our colleges and praise it in the media. On top of its evil history of crime, collectivism inevitably plunges the country that embraces it into poverty. Look at the economic ruins of Venezuela, Nicaragua, Cuba and Zimbabwe. They are proof of the far left's refusal to learn from its failures. If results matter, this doctrine should be put to rest.

Author Richard Ebeling writes, "It is amazing how short humanity's historical memory can be. Listening to some in American academia and on social media, you would think that socialism was a bright, new, and shiny idea never tried before that promises a beautiful future of peace, love, and bountifulness for all. It is as if a hundred years of socialism in countries around the world had never happened.

"If the reality of actual socialism in the 20th century is brought up, many 'progressives' and 'democratic' socialists respond by insisting that none of these historical episodes were instances of 'real' socialism. It was just that the wrong people had been in charge, or it had not been implemented in the right way, or political circumstances had prevented it from getting a 'fair chance' of successfully working, or it is all lies or exaggerations about the supposed 'bad' or 'harsh' experiences under these socialist regimes. You cannot blame socialism for there having been a Lenin, or a Stalin, or a Chairman Mao, or a Fidel Castro, or a Kim Il-Sung, or a Pol Pot, or a Hugo Chavez.

"Tyranny, terror, mass murder, and economic stagnation, along with political plunder and privilege for the few at the top of socialist government hierarchies were not indicative of what socialism could be. Just give it one more chance. And, then, another chance, and another.

"What a world was that of socialism-in-practice! A world of what the Austrian economist, Ludwig von Mises, titled one of his shorter books, *Planned Chaos* (1947). But even more, Soviet socialism was an upside-down Alice-in-Wonderland-Through-the-Looking-Glass world of literal planned madness. When the French sociologist, Gustave Le Bon published *The Psychology of Socialism* in 1899, he feared that, 'One nation, at least, will have to suffer it [the establishment of a socialist system] for the instruction of the world.' Is it really necessary to go through it all again? Let us hope not."

I don't remember while growing up that business leaders were Democrats. For the most part they were Republicans. They universally stood against high taxes, big government, social welfare and too much regulation. They strongly advocated capitalism and a government that balanced budgets. They opposed Lyndon Johnson's Great Society programs and the inroads of the Warren Court. They had no patience with socialism and communism which they saw as evil.

Today it seems that the founders of our most successful companies are liberals. Amazon, Starbucks, Microsoft, Apple, and Costco are but a few. It used to be that the explanation for a company founder being a Democrat was that he or she wanted to encourage regulations that eliminated competitors. Once a company got big enough they could use the political system to pass laws and other requirements that barred new companies from competing with them.

That's unlikely to be the case today. The company founders and billionaires of today who are leftists have a different motivation. Your guess is as good as mine as to why. My theory is that it's a result of the struggle to overcome racism in the 1960s. This social revolution that elevated blacks to full equality had a profound impact on people. Their indignation over the events in Little Rock and Birmingham turned them into liberals on this issue. Although the pendulum has swung back, to this day the issue of racism remains on the front burner. Many of us believe that this issue has been redressed, but in the schools, the media and the institutions it still burns bright. The college-educated entrepreneurs of today often become liberals before they think much about free markets and enterprise.

The sad part about all this is that the left wants to enact laws that cripple capitalism. They want to strip successful companies of their capital and hamstring business with planning and intervention. Rich, successful liberals are like liberals everywhere, they believe in their socialist dogma so deeply they ignore the negative results. They can't be made to see that liberal policies are destructive and ruinous. Our country cannot persist in its greatness if the left remains so influential. As for our Silicone Valley liberals, they are providing the government the rope with which to hang them.

Philosopher M. N. Gordon extrapolates, "'The way to Hell is paved with good intentions,' remarked Karl Marx in *Das Kapital*. The devious fellow was bemoaning evil capitalists for having the gall to use their own money for the express purpose of making more money. Marx, a rambling busybody, was habitually wrong. The road to hell is paved with something much more than good intentions. Grift, graft, larceny, corruption and fake money are what primarily composes the pavement. Good intentions are merely dusted in to better the aesthetic. If you want to understand what's going on with exploding price inflation then you must understand this. Right now in the United States we have a currency that's controlled by central planners. Specifically, we have what Marx envisioned in Plank No. 5 of his Communist Manifesto: 'No. 5. Centralization of credit in the hands of the state, by means of a national bank with state capital and an exclusive monopoly.'

"The Federal Reserve System, created by the Federal Reserve Act of Congress in 1913, is indeed a 'national bank' and it politically manipulates interest rates and holds a monopoly on legal counterfeiting in the United States. Without the Fed's policies of mass credit creation the U.S. government could have never run up a national debt over $28 trillion. Without the Fed's policies of extreme credit market intervention the U.S. trade deficit for March of $74.4 billion – a new record – would have never been possible. Without the Fed's printing press money the U.S. government could have never run annual budget deficits over $3 trillion. The fact is centralized credit in the hands of a central bank always leads to money supply inflation. Asset price inflation and consumer price inflation then follow in strange and unpredictable ways. These price distortions are not defects of capitalism. They're symptoms of a scam currency managed by central planners.

"Indeed, the results of government intervention are always the same. Stagnation, inflation, declining living standards, and widespread social disorder. No doubt, they'll be repeated to insanity. True capitalism requires an honest currency and market-determined pricing. Remember this in the weeks to come. As prices rise, politicians and central planners – people like Alexandria Ocasio-Cortez and Janet Yellen – will look to pin inflation on evil capitalists and price gouging business owners. Don't believe their lies. Just follow the fake money back to its origin. There you'll find the Fed, hard at work, applying the pavement to Karl Marx's road to hell. Buckle up!"

Once leftists take over a country through elections or revolutions, constitutional protections are quickly eliminated. Those who resist are imprisoned or murdered. That, of course, is the lesson of history. But today's youthful crew of Bernie Sanders followers pay no heed to history. If a belief in socialism spreads to underclass voters and incites the criminals among them, we shall all have reason to fear. No other political idea ever spread so far, so fast or created such misery and failure. However, the New York Times wrote that the collapse of communism in Russia thirty years ago could be the source of socialism's renewal. Granted, we are a long way from electing a socialist government, but so were the Venezuelans and most countries (including the U.S.) are slowly evolving into socialism.

Pope Pius XI wrote in 1931, "Communism teaches and seeks two objectives: unrelenting class warfare and the complete eradication of private ownership. Not secretly or by hidden methods does it do this, but publicly, openly, and by employing any means possible, even the most violent. To achieve these objectives there is nothing it is afraid to do, nothing for which it has respect or reverence. When it comes to power, it is ferocious in its cruelty and inhumanity. The horrible slaughter and destruction through which it has laid waste to vast regions of Eastern Europe and Asia give evidence of this."

Author Simon Black wrote, "This willful ignorance of the undercurrent coursing its way through the Western world will not save anyone from the destruction it brings. For example, 'peaceful protesters' in Portland, Oregon celebrated Columbus Day with an 'Indigenous People's Day of Rage.' They weren't even pretending to be peaceful. They called it what it is: RAGE. That's literally the name they gave to their own actions. Hundreds of people dressed in all black, covered their faces, and armed themselves with shields and nightsticks. They marched their way through the city, smashed windows, and forced any witnesses to stop filming and delete photographs. The protesters tore down statues of Teddy Roosevelt and Abraham Lincoln. They smashed the windows of the Oregon Historical Society building, and unfurled a banner that said "stop honoring racist colonizer murderers." Police did not even attempt to intervene until the rioters had been on the streets for hours and had caused havoc and destruction.

"Ironically, much of the mainstream media still refuses to acknowledge that this group 'Antifa'– the fascists who call themselves anti-fascists – even exists. It's obvious that a small, fringe, ideological minority has started to take control. They have squashed civil discourse and free speech. Dissent is met with violence and intimidation. And if you dare to speak out, you become a target. That could mean being 'cancelled' by the Twitter mob or being accosted in public. Several people have already been killed in protests across the nation. When people like the former CEO of Twitter are calling for capitalists to be 'lined up against the wall and shot,' it's time to take the threat seriously.

"This is far from the first time in history that a tiny fraction of the population has resorted to violence and extremism to force their agenda on a nation. But you don't have to watch helplessly as the born-again Brownshirts destroy everything you have worked for. The first step is to recognize that the radical movement will not simply go away on its own. This has been growing for some time, and history tells us that it could become much worse. Second, have a rock solid Plan B. This means deciding – in advance, when you're still calm and rational – what steps to take in order to secure your family's safety, your prosperity, and your freedom in a worst-case scenario. After all, you don't want to be thinking about your next move when some Antifa thug hurls a Molotov cocktail through your window."

Antifa hopes to eliminate capitalism. Many on the left agree. The Minneapolis Star Tribune (a left-wing newspaper) featured a quote on the Sunday editorial page that claims without intensive regulation "capitalism is a menace to society." That kind of regulation is called interventionism. It closely resembles socialism and collectivism. Its proponents forget that unbridled capitalism eliminated starvation within the U.S. and greatly extended lifetimes. Capitalism and progress are synonymous. Socialism and starvation are also synonymous but that doesn't register with the radicals. In Cuba, the people yearn to be free of the Communists. Our media quickly forgot the recent outbreak of dissatisfaction from the Cuban people. The left never lets real life events change their views. That's why the liberal media refuses to honestly report on the plight of the Cuban people.

Liberals like to claim they are not socialists. However, they want the government to run things and control the free market. Unfortunately, there is no half-way between capitalism and socialism. There is only a gradual transition from capitalism to socialism. The mixed economy is a slippery slope to big government and collectivism.

The great economist Ludwig von Mises stated succinctly, "Capitalism is essentially a system of mass production for the satisfaction of the needs of the masses. It pours a horn of plenty upon the common man. It has raised the average standard of living to a height never dreamed of in earlier years. It has made accessible to millions of people enjoyments which a few generations ago were only within the reach of a small elite...Capitalism needs neither propaganda nor apostles. Its achievements speak for themselves. Capitalism delivers the goods.... The issue is always the same: the government or the market. There is no third solution... A society that chooses between capitalism and socialism does not choose between two social systems; it chooses between social cooperation and the disintegration of society. Socialism is not an alternative to capitalism; it is an alternative to any system under which men can live as human beings."

Economist Germinal G. Van writes about Africa's experience with collectivism, "Socialism has failed wherever it was tried, and the African countries that have experimented with socialism were not exempted from its failure. The undeniable fact remains that Africa has the lowest living standard compared to the rest of the world because socialism has impoverished the African continent. In the 1960s, many African countries embraced socialism as their economic and political system. These countries became significantly worse off by the 1980s.

"Socialism had utterly stagnated the economies of these countries until a market economy was once again reinstated. What Africans have failed to grasp about capitalism and the free market is that, it is not a system intrinsic to Western culture. It is a system intrinsic to human nature regardless of race, ethnicity, or the local culture. Socialism has failed in Africa as it has failed in Eastern Europe, India, China and in South America. The pursuit of one's self-interests is an intrinsic factor of human nature that no central authority can change regardless of the goal of the common good."

Recently, I noticed a photo of young Marxists holding up a variety of signs as they marched in a demonstration. One sign said, "Join the Struggle against Capitalism." Another sign said, "Free Education, Funded by Expropriation." To me the latter sign is the essence of the left; they want your money. They want what you own and they want your affluent lifestyle. They are secretly and deeply infected with envy. They want the things you paid a price for, but they want them without a price. They want to body slam you and bring you down to earth. Equality doesn't interest them, they want the upper hand.

Some Democrats might disagree with these communists, but they don't hesitate to vote for candidates who echo Marxists sentiments. In that sense, liberals are the "useful idiots" that Lenin described during the Russian revolution. The people who sided with the Reds never thought that all the wealth would be confiscated by the Bolsheviks or that they would shoot the Czar and his lovely family. Affairs in Russia just kept sliding leftward until their constitution became a broken promise and the rich were murdered along with anyone else who disagreed.

Revolutions and other great social changes are often triggered by economic declines. Socialism always grows in depressions. We are one or two Supreme Court judges and a handful of legislators away from watering down the Constitution and beginning the high-tax regime that evolves into expropriation. Marxists preach our overthrow in the universities and leftists whip up race, class and gender hatreds that poison our discourse. Magazines, newspapers, movies, television and radio are solidly socialist. Our greatest generations (mine included) are no longer a bulwark against the commies and we cannot replace them. You have to wonder if liberals ever read history and if they do, does it register? In any case, the coming bitter history lesson is one I probably won't be around for, but unfortunately my kids and grandkids will.

Author Brandon Smith writes, "Leftists and Marxists think that equality of opportunity is not enough. They think that there should also be equality of outcome. This delusion sits at the core of all Marxist thinking. Equality of outcome is impossible because not all people are born equal. Some people are, frankly, born superior to others. Some people are born smarter. Some people are born stronger, taller and faster. Some people are born with innate musical or artistic talent. Some people are born with innate mathematical understanding.

"The psychological reality of mankind is that we are not born as blank slates; we are born with inherent qualities and the seeds of unique individual talents. Marxists suffer from a mental disconnect with this concept. If they were to admit that people are born with individual qualities and advantages and are not blank slates, then the foundation of their philosophy falls apart. They think people must be reeducated to reject bad beliefs and bad habits they were taught as children and learn to accept that everyone starts life out exactly the same. Therefore, the majority of people who succeed are those that were given an unfair advantage, and success should be treated with disdain and suspicion."

The left constantly claims that our successful economic system is evil and unjust. They want to eliminate the free market and replace it with interventionism. They want to break up the largest and most successful companies and put unions into company management. They are mounting a global warming hysteria in order to gain control of energy policies. The late Joseph Sobran explained it perfectly. "Liberalism's fatal flaw is that it has no permanent norms, only a succession of enthusiasms espoused by minor prophets. Each of these seems like a hot new idea to liberals, but soon goes to irksome and destructive extremes."

Daniel Henninger wrote, "Decades ago, progressives pushed the unprecedented social experiment known as deinstitutionalization of the severely mentally ill. Hospital beds were never replaced. Promised off-site care eroded. It is a massive policy failure, with many of these abandoned, mostly male patients destructively self-medicating on the street with alcohol and heroin. The chance of reversing this progressive experiment is about zero. They'll let it rip. Urban crime? The solution is more of the same failure: defund the police, deinstitutionalize prisons and pursue de minimis prosecution. Their promised replacements – psychologists and social workers – will never materialize. Today, urban neighborhoods are beset with the abandoned mentally ill and the unrestrained, conscienceless violence of young men in gangs."

Author Alyssa Ahlgren expounds, "I'm sitting in a small coffee shop (in Minneapolis) trying to think of what to write about. I scroll through my newsfeed on my phone looking at the latest headlines of Democratic candidates calling for policies to 'fix' the so-called injustices of capitalism. I put my phone down and continue to look around. I see people talking freely, working on their MacBooks, ordering food they get in an instant, seeing cars go by outside, and it dawned on me. We live in the most privileged time in the most prosperous nation and we've become completely blind to it. Vehicles, food, technology, freedom to associate with whom we choose. These things are so ingrained in our American way of life we don't give them a second thought. We are so well off here in the United States that our poverty line begins 31 times above the global average. Thirty. One. Times. Virtually no one in the United States is considered poor by global standards. Yet, in a time where we can order a product off Amazon with one click and have it at our doorstep the next day, we are unappreciative, unsatisfied, and ungrateful.

"Our non-appreciation is evident as the popularity of socialist policies among my generation continues to grow. Democratic Congresswoman Alexandria Ocasio-Cortez recently said to Newsweek talking about the millennial generation, 'An entire generation, which is now becoming one of the largest electorates in America, came of age and never saw American prosperity.' Never saw American prosperity! Let that sink in. When I first read that statement, I thought to myself, this was quite literally the most entitled and factually illiterate thing I've ever heard in my 26 years on this earth. Many young people agree with her, which is entirely misguided. My generation is being indoctrinated by a mainstream narrative to actually believe we have never seen prosperity. I know this first-hand, I went to college, let's just say I didn't have the popular opinion.

"Why then, with all of the overwhelming evidence around us, evidence that I can even see sitting at a coffee shop, do we not view this as prosperity? We have people who are dying to get into our country. People around the world destitute and truly impoverished. Yet, we have a young generation convinced they've never seen prosperity, and as a result, elect politicians dead set on taking steps towards abolishing capitalism.

"Why? The answer is this; my generation has only seen prosperity. We have no contrast. We didn't live in the Great Depression, or live through two world wars, the Korean War, The Vietnam War or see the rise and fall of socialism and communism. We don't know what it's like to live without the internet, without cars, without smartphones. We don't have a lack of prosperity problem. We have an entitlement problem, an ungratefulness problem, and it's spreading like a plague."

These leftists are the most negative people on earth. They always have a hot-button issue that's a perceived injustice or a social wrong that must be corrected. They dislike the U.S., the one country in the world that has dramatically rolled back discrimination and lifted millions out of poverty. Karl Marx was the same kind of pessimist. Instead of seeing the laboring class working their way towards a better life he saw them being cheated and trampled. Today's radicals see injustice everywhere. They never look at the bright side of things or ever see the benefits and luxuries showered upon us by capitalism.

The left fails to understand that the free market is no more than the buying choices of the people. In the market economy the consumers are the kings and queens. Their buying decisions determine what companies succeed or fail. Any interference by the government means a reduction of buying choices. That's another way of saying reduced freedoms. To succeed capitalists must strive to meet the needs of the consumer. Their motives may well be selfish but the consumers are merciless and they must serve them well or perish. It's as near to a perfect system as humanity will ever achieve. Unfortunately, these days we have more socialism than capitalism and the market economy gets blamed for the sorry results of government intervention.

The left-wing proponents who denigrate capitalism must wear blinders. In the entire history of socialism they haven't been able to create a single commercial innovation. Meanwhile, capitalism has showered us with so many material blessings we can't keep track of them. In the 19th century, 50% of the children born would not live to adulthood. Capitalism dramatically extends lifespans, provides opportunities, work and success. As professor Mises so clearly instructed, "If you seek its monument, look around you."

I read a lot of books about the Second World War, especially the struggle on the eastern front between Russia and Germany. Nothing compares to the ferocity, scope and duration of that struggle. The U.S.A. lost almost 300,000 soldiers in WWII fighting Japan and Germany. The Russians had 12 to 14 million soldiers killed fighting Germany. There are quite a few books and personal accounts written by German soldiers, but not many by Russians. So, I was glad to get a copy of *Tank Rider* just published this year in the U.S. The author rode tanks from 1943 to 1945 as a 20-year-old lieutenant through some of the fiercest battles in Russia and Germany. He wrote the book years after the war was over, but his memory was still sharp.

Books like this also give you insight into the culture and the living conditions inside Russia at the time. One thing that stands out is the lack of food and physical comforts. In the late 1930s, the author often went hungry and slept on the floor without blankets. As a recruit he sometimes had nothing more than a single beet in boiled water for a day's nourishment. Finding something to eat became an obsession. As the war unfolded, the Russian army had to live off the land taking food from civilians or from captured German supplies. The point is that under communism, Russia couldn't feed its people or even sustain its army. Russian communism led to starvation and poverty.

A current example of starvation under communism exists in Venezuela. Shortages of food have reduced the population to eating flamingos, anteaters and donkeys. This once prosperous country has descended into socialist hell and the people are fleeing. When you dismantle capitalism, your citizens begin to starve. Nevertheless, half the people in America cannot connect the dots. They see capitalism as evil or unworkable. They want to replace it with a government-controlled system. In other words, they favor socialism over capitalism. This is a form of national suicide. Its advocates are strongest in the media, the campuses, Hollywood, New York City, Silicon Valley, and other liberal bastions. If they had a few weeks on 200 calories a day, they would see things differently. But by the time that happens, it will be too late.

CHAPTER EIGHT
MMT: CRACKPOT THEORY

"Continued inflation inevitability leads to catastrophe."
~Ludwig von Mises

"The Federal Reserve and the banking system it controls have created massive levels of unsupportable debt that now weighs down all sectors of the economy. In the next crisis much of this debt will default, and take down the financial system as it does."
~Mark J. Lundeen

"Liberal dominance of important areas of America's social and political life has undermined many of the virtues that have sustained this country."
~Mona Charen

Modern Monetary Theory (MMT) is the process of giving people free money they didn't earn. This free money has two serious consequences for our country. It ruins the character of those who come to rely on it and its constant expansion unleashes powerful financial and monetary trends that threaten the dollar, the markets, and our economy. These are terrible problems. For example, the current outbreak of crime can be linked to free money. For seventy years, the government has been pumping billions of dollars into the high crime areas of our major cities. It hasn't helped, they are worse than ever. Welfare money may initially be helpful and beneficial, but as it becomes permanent, the dependency and boredom it creates promote mischief. Free money leads to alcoholism, addiction, crime, worsening poverty and even homelessness. Almost all of the street people get free money from welfare and Social Security Disability, much of which goes to pay for their expensive narcotics. You can also blame free money for contributing to the rash of deaths that come from drug overdoses.

The liberals and leftists are quick to blame the plight of the underclass on racism and historical inequities. Some of that is true, but it's also true that minority families were growing stronger financially and were more united until the welfare explosion of the 1960s. That caused families to disintegrate and dependency to replace work and self-reliance. Richard Vedder and Braden Colegrove wrote in the Wall Street Journal, "Expanded government entitlements following the Great Society era have reduced traditional family formation, reduced incentives to excel both in school and on the job, and increased crime."

Up until a few years ago, immigrants who came to America got little from the government. Now these newcomers are immediately given free money. While some of this is necessary, free money serves as a great incentive to come to America. Liberals favor wide-open borders because indigenous people and Hispanics tend to support leftists with their votes. Millions more will be coming if the money holds out and the border stays open. Free money is the principal cause of the immigration crisis.

Lately, TV commercials have been advocating that people contact government offices to get free stuff including hearing aids and free dentistry. Then there is the push for free tuition, loan forgiveness, free daycare, free healthcare and guaranteed income payments. That's on top of billions of subsidies already in existence. At election time, voters that are getting this free money are certain to vote for politicians who favor more subsidies. In other words, free money leads to socialism and that is its greatest sin.

It's hard to imagine a financial idea more reckless than Modern Monetary Theory (MMT). What follows are a number of expert opinions on why it's a bad idea.

Author James Gorrie tells us, "'As long as the government can print money, we'll never be broke.' That's the idea behind modern monetary theory (MMT) in a nutshell. Naturally, many of the nuts in Washington are starting to get behind this unhinged notion. That includes members of Congress such as Rep. Alexandria Ocasio-Cortez (D-N.Y.) and Democrat Sen. Elizabeth Warren (D-Mass.).

"Sure, a cluster of economists in and around Wall Street and Washington, D.C. are pushing this very dangerous set of policies that are dressed up in academic terminology such as 'neo-Keynesianism' so that they sound almost sane. But MMT is as far from economic sanity as one can get. But let's face it, Wall Street loves any idea that puts money into the market. In essence, the main idea behind MMT is that any government spending can be paid for with printed money. An in-depth look into history shows that the absurd idea of printing unlimited amounts of money leads a nation into hyperinflation and economic ruin.

"Money is a store of value. In the absence of tangible backing such as gold, the issuing country and the strength of its economy are the main drivers of acceptance of a currency, both domestically and internationally. Moreover, perception is reality. In the case of the United States, MMT spending doesn't happen in a vacuum. Other nations have to adjust their currency levels to ours. That means the United States would be exporting inflation. What nation will accept U.S. dollars – the world's reserve currency – if it's saddled with an infinite level of debt and the very real prospect of hyperinflation at any time? The answer is very few, if any. What's more, competitor nations such as Russia and China would be tempted to help break the dollar by backing or partially backing their currency – or a basket of currencies – with gold. That would be the end of the dollar and the U.S. economy as we know it."

Financial editor Fred Hickey writes, "A green light has been given politicians in Washington D.C. to spend at levels this country has never seen before, knowing the Fed will continue to monetize the massively growing deficits. There seems to be no limit to how much the politicians want to spend. Many of them have swallowed the crackpot Modern Monetary Theory (MMT) hook, line and sinker. Some people refer to the MMT as the 'Magic Money Tree.' Last week 21 Senate Democrats wrote to President Biden urging him to include recurring direct payments and further extensions of jobless benefits in his economic recovery plans. We're getting perilously close to UBI (Universal Basic Income) payments.

"Though Fed Chairman Powell said that the Fed remained strongly committed to keeping the public's expectations for future price increases under control, that's becoming an increasingly onerous task. The Bureau of Labor Statistics (BLS) will continue to pump out their suppressed inflation figures every month (thoroughly cooked with 'hedonic' adjustments, ridiculous calculations of imputed rents, etc.), but the public can see with their own eyes the climbing gasoline prices at the pump, the surging food prices, the out-of-control housing bubble, rising new and used auto and truck prices (and reduced discounts), soaring costs of lumber (almost tripling) for their home improvement projects, higher prices for goods using steel (refrigerators, washing machines, gas grills), plastics, paper products and more."

Author Jim Rickards wrote, "For those unfamiliar with MMT, it says that the U.S. can spend as much as it wants, borrow to cover the deficits and monetize the debt with Fed money-printing. The 'theory' is not much of a theory because it lacks evidence, and there's nothing 'modern' about it because it has been around for over 100 years. Still, it is all the rage in Washington, D.C. these days.

"MMT has three basic tenets. The first is to treat the Treasury and the Fed as a single entity with a single balance sheet. Legally, the two institutions are completely separate, but MMT insists that government can merge Treasury and Fed operations into a single engine for spending, borrowing and printing. The second idea is that citizens must accept dollars (whether they like it or not) because you need dollars to pay taxes, and if you don't pay taxes, you'll go to jail. The third idea is that there is no practical limit to how much debt the U.S. can issue.

"MMT is a disaster in the making (although it may take a few years to play out). It's OK to borrow money if you invest in highly productive assets. But, if you just spend the money to support a stagnant economy with handouts, you're simply digging a deeper debt hole for yourself. Multi-trillion dollar deficit spending plans will emerge soon from the new Congress. The Treasury will spend the money. The Fed will buy the Treasury debt with newly-printed money. Eventually, you end up with inflation, higher interest rates, higher taxes, default or all of the above. The U.S. will go broke. It's not quite the rosy scenario the MMT crowd would have you believe."

Editor Peter Krauth explained, "MMT is the idea that federal spending is not limited by revenues: printing money is a tool to be used to help a country deal with its economic issues, and that it will not automatically trigger inflation or currency devaluation. Proponents believe governments who print and spend their own currency should not be limited in their spending to avoid deficits and a growing debt. They say deficits and debt don't matter unless they begin generating inflation.

"It needs to be pointed out here that this is a departure from the way the rest of the world works. A company or an individual cannot operate on that basis. Firstly, they don't print their own money and so they don't have that luxury. They also cannot borrow to infinity because at some point creditors will force them into bankruptcy. That exact scenario can't happen with a country, because MMT says it can just keep printing to pay for spending and to pay interest on debts. But in fact, it's a vicious circle in which the public eventually loses confidence.

"One thing to keep in mind is that central banks only control short term rates. For the most part, long term rates are determined by the market. And that's where inflation fears will often show up first. That's likely what we've been witnessing over the last several months in U.S. long-term Treasuries, whose yields have risen dramatically. In effect, the market is saying those bonds are now worth less, which pushes up their yields, as it senses higher inflation on the horizon.

"And it's why we've seen commodities like gold and silver rise in the past year. It's also why we've seen shortages, delivery delays, and huge premiums on coins and bullion bars at precious metals dealers. People are catching on, and they are trading their fiat currency for things of inherent value. The way I see it, MMT is going to be popular with future governments as they come to see the potential of limitless spending on all their favorite pet projects. The masses, despite little understanding, will come to accept MMT as a great new economic approach that will allow them to get all the 'goodies' that governments will be happy to provide, in return for votes. In the end, it's important for you to know MMT will only exacerbate and accelerate the overspending problems we have today. So now that you hopefully understand MMT a bit better, and how it's supposed to work, you can see it with a more critical eye. And you can also better prepare for its inevitable effect of driving precious metals and commodities much, much higher."

Author Doug Casey says, "Modern Monetary Theory (MMT) centers around the notion that the economy in general, and money in particular, should be the creatures of the State. MMT basically posits that the wise and incorruptible solons in government should create as much currency as they think is needed, spend it in areas they like, and solve any problems that occur with more laws and regulations.

"These schemes have never worked in all of history. They result in a vastly lower standard of living, along with social strife. MMT is about radically increased government control. The argument shouldn't be over whether MMT will 'work' or not. The argument should be about whether it's moral and proper for people in the government – whether elected or appointed – to print money to change the economy into something that suits them better.

"This matter is essentially a moral question, not a technical question. Does somebody in government have a right to determine your economic destiny? Or not? The fact that Alexandria Ocasio-Cortez – an ambitious, terminally ignorant, morally crippled 31-year-old bartender – is setting the tone for this whole discussion tells you how degraded the U.S. has become. It's well on its way to turning into a giant welfare and police state. I always look on the bright side. Which is that – if you give yourself a little psychological distance – this is all a comedy."

Author Michael Snyder wrote, "We crossed a line that should have never been crossed when we sent 'stimulus payments' directly to the American people during the very early stages of the Covid-19 pandemic. Even many Republicans that supported the measure acknowledged that what they were doing was pure socialism, but they defended the payments by insisting that we were in the middle of a major national emergency. At the time, I warned that once the government started issuing such checks, the American people would always keep demanding more. When it was announced that the latest round of 'stimulus payments' would only be $600 per person, angry activists vandalized Nancy Pelosi's house. Of course they got Mitch McConnell's house too. In both cases, the vandals made it exceedingly clear that they wanted more government money. Sadly, it wasn't just a handful of activists that went ballistic. Literally millions of enraged Americans posted angry messages on social media that expressed how 'insulting' the $600 figure was.

"But prior to this pandemic, the U.S. government had never sent out 'universal basic income' checks in the entire history of our country. So you would think that most people should be grateful for an extra $600, but instead there was a tremendous amount of rage. Benjamin Franklin once made the following statement: 'When the people find that they can vote themselves money that will herald the end of the republic.'"

Senator Rand Paul said this recently on the Senate floor: "The monstrous spending bill presented today is not just a 'deficits don't matter' disaster; it is everything Republicans say they don't believe in. This bill is free money for everyone. Proponents don't care if you're fully employed or own your own house or own your own business. 'Free money for everyone,' they cry.

"And yet if free money were the answer, if money really grew on trees, why not give more free money? Why not give it out all the time? Why stop at $600 a person? Why not $1,000? Why not $2,000? Maybe these new 'free money Republicans' should join the 'everybody gets a guaranteed income' caucus. Why not $20,000 a year for everybody? Why not $30,000? If we can print up money with impunity, why not do it? The Treasury can just keep printing the money. That is, until someone points out that the emperor has no clothes and that the dollar no longer has value."

CHAPTER NINE
TAXES

"Why raise a tax rate that would reduce investment, reduce wage growth and reduce revenue for the government? Temporary economic insanity is one possible explanation. Another is punishment for its own sake. This is what happens when you turn your economic policy over to Bernie Sanders and Elizabeth Warren."
~Wall Street Journal

"The idea that jobs, businesses and wealth follow low tax rates is widely accepted."
~Stephen Moore

My friend Joe, who lives in Illinois, is making plans to move elsewhere. Income tax rates on high earners are going up, and a host of other tax hikes are under consideration in Illinois. Cities and states run by liberals inevitably go over their budget because of social spending. To pay for these social schemes they have to raise taxes.

Author Mark Glennor provides a rundown on proposed new taxes in Illinois: "Gas tax hike, vehicle registration fee hike, new ridesharing tax of $1 per ride, expanding Chicago's 'Netflix tax' – a 7% tax on users of streaming services, cable and satellite customers, higher taxes on beer, wine and liquor, new statewide parking garage tax, doubling the real estate transfer tax, higher registration fees for electric vehicles, a plastic tax, tax on Medicaid providers, sports gambling tax, marijuana tax, video gambling tax, retailer tax hike, e-cigarette tax hike, and higher cigarette taxes."

The Democratic Party only knows how to raise taxes, add taxes, increase fees, add regulations, impose fines, confiscate assets, increase penalties and add licensing requirements. Illinois is in dire financial straits. All these progressive tax schemes will make matters worse and more people will leave the state.

Upon listening to recent Democratic speeches it occurred to me that if Marx, Lenin, Castro and Che Guevara were talking they would sound much the same. Their unifying theme is hostility towards the rich and raising taxes. They despise capitalism and free markets. Most of all they want to get their hands on the money that affluent people have. A Democratic administration will invariably be an orgy of tax gouging and anti-business initiatives. The great Austrian economist Ludwig von Mises explained the left's motivation this way: "Nothing is more calculated to make a demagogue popular than a constantly reiterated demand for heavy taxes on the rich. Capital levies and high income taxes on the larger incomes are extraordinarily popular with the masses, who do not have to pay them."

Analyst Graham Summers writes, "We are now deep into a propaganda campaign to convince the American public that it's time for wealth taxes and cash grabs. In a nutshell, the argument is that the government is running a huge deficit. There is too much debt. So, the way to fix this is a wealth tax. A month ago, the IMF published a paper stating that governments should consider increasing taxes on: 1) Income, 2) Property, and 3) Wealth. The IMF claims this should be seen as a 'Solidarity Surcharge,' a kind of 'we're all in this together' campaign to help economies.

We will be seeing more and more calls for wealth taxes from the mainstream media. The Washington Post, The Financial Times, Politico, The Guardian and others are already pushing the narrative that it's about making the super-rich 'pay their fair share' or 'helping out those less fortunate.' However, the reality is that the real plan the IMF is pushing involves a 10% wealth tax on net wealth for everyone who has it. "Put another way, anyone who owns more asserts than debt, should pay out 10% of that amount in wealth taxes. The goal is to find new sources of capital to plug the massive debt holes created by bailouts and other stimulus efforts."

Is anybody getting poorer in America? You would think that our people are falling into poverty and hard times when liberal politicians speak. It's just the opposite. We're all doing better. Yes, billionaires are getting richer, but that's not taking anything away from anybody.

Actually, the money that the wealthy have creates employment and prosperity. It's not a zero-sum game as many socialists believe. If you get a dollar richer, nobody gets a dollar poorer because of it. In fact, the wealthiest countries where living standards are the highest have the most millionaires and billionaires.

Taxing the money away from the rich hurts the economy and increases unemployment. The left wants that money to fund their giveaways. They are motivated by a runaway social sympathy that's beyond impractical. They have done incalculable damage to the people they subsidize. Yet they want to give more money in hopes of solving the festering moral and behavioral problems they've created. The liberals are intent on giving the people a free ride rather than have them solve their problems with resourcefulness and diligence. They want to use the money that working people earn in ways that weaken the populace and foster anti-social behavior. If they get the upper hand for a lengthy period of time, America will hit the gutter as surely as intoxicated druggies on California streets.

Author Bradley Thomas wrote, "A mantra popularized by Bernie Sanders and like-minded progressives declares 'billionaires should not exist.' The statement serves as both a declaration of the 'immorality' of wealth inequality as well as a justification for steep confiscatory taxes on wealth favored by the likes of Sanders and Elizabeth Warren.

"As Ludwig von Mises pointed out in *Human Action*, confiscatory taxes on the wealthy may indeed cause billionaires to be slightly worse off, but the rest of us will be harmed more severely. He wrote that such a law 'restricts the activities of precisely those entrepreneurs who are most successful in filling the wants of consumers.' Under such confiscatory taxation, Mises continued, '(M)any who are multimillionaires today would live in more modest circumstances. But all those new branches of industry which supply the masses with articles unheard of before would operate, if at all, on a much smaller scale, and their products would be beyond the reach of the common man.'

"Greater productivity is made possible only through a greater investment of capital per capita, so when the accumulation of capital is stunted by confiscatory taxes, the amount of goods and services being brought to the market is smaller than it could otherwise be. As goods become more scarce, they become out of reach for average and lower-income households. Common household items we take for granted, like air conditioning, internet connection, computers, and smartphones would remain luxury goods accessible only to the already rich.

"The desire by some to impose confiscatory taxes on the wealthy is driven largely by an envy that blinds them to the fact that such taxes would end up hurting the common man much more than the billionaires. Moreover, the taxes could serve to protect the already wealthy from competition and hamper economic progress. It may be emotionally satisfying for many to favor sticking it to billionaires, but reason informs us that in so doing it is the poor who would end up paying the steepest price."

Henry Hazlitt (1894-1993) was a brilliant economic thinker and columnist for Newsweek and The New York Times (before they were socialists). He penned these words on taxes: "Certainly there is no evidence that the steeply progressive tax rates have helped the poor. On the contrary, these confiscatory rates clearly undermine incentives, reduce production and capital accumulation, and leave less to be shared by everybody. By striking directly at new investment, the present corporate income tax slows down economic growth more directly and surely than does any other tax. The tax, by hurting business and investment, hurts employment and slows down the increase in productivity and in real wages. In brief, in the long run it hurts most of all the mass of the country's workers."

Apparently, Mr. Hazlitt could see the future because many years ago he wrote about guaranteed incomes and negative taxes, "The guaranteed-income plan would lead to wholesale idleness and pauperization among nearly all those earning less than the minimum wage, and among many earning just a little more. But in addition to the erosion of the incentive to work, there would be just as serious an erosion of the incentive to save. The main reason most people save is to meet possible but unforeseeable contingencies, such as illness, accidents, or the loss of a job. If everyone were guaranteed a minimum cash income by the government, this main incentive for saving would disappear. The important habit of saving might disappear with it. The more affluent minority, it is true, also save toward a retirement income in old age or for supplementary income in their working years. But with the prevalence of a guaranteed-income system, this type of saving also would be profoundly discouraged. This would be certain to mean a reduction in both the nation's capital accumulation and the investment in more and new and better tools, plants and equipment upon which all of us depend for increased national productivity, increased real wages, more lucrative employment, and economic progress in general. We might even enter an era of net capital consumption. In other words, the long-term effect of a guaranteed-income plan would be to increase poverty, not to reduce it.

"It is important to point out that to be concerned with the destructive effects of a guaranteed-income program on the incentives of people to work and save, is not to pass a wholesale moral judgment on the present poor. We must avoid on the one hand the sweeping assumption, sometimes made by conservatives, that the poor have no one to blame for their poverty but themselves, and yet resist on the other hand the frequent sweeping 'liberal' assumption that all the poor or jobless are poor or jobless 'through no fault of their own.' The only realistic presumption is that some people are poor or jobless through no fault of their own, that some are poor or jobless entirely through fault of their own, but that the great majority are poor or jobless through various complicated mixtures of misfortune and personal mistakes or shortcomings. The distinction between those who are trying to cure their poverty by their own efforts, and those who are not, is vital for any workable solution of the problem of poverty. The central vice is that they ignore this distinction. The result of all the guaranteed-income and 'negative income tax' schemes is that these schemes would destroy incentives on a wholesale scale, and therefore have the opposite of their intended effect."

To a large extent much of what Mr. Hazlitt warned against has already happened. However, it can get worse. The left wants income taxes as high as 60% with no deductions. They want capital gains taxes to be replaced at regular income tax rates. Estate taxes could also be raised to punitive levels. The socialist dream of a tax on wealth may also be around the corner. By voting in a liberal majority in Congress, the left will be able to raise taxes to confiscatory levels and reward their constituents with the money.

Author Anthony Davies writes, "For years, politicians have claimed that the rich weren't paying their 'fair share.' While it's taken a decade or more for voters to catch wind of the truth, people are finally beginning to realize that the rich actually pay far more than the rest of us. According to Congressional Budget Office figures, the average household in the top one percent earns 120 times what the average poor household earns, but pays 2,000 times the taxes. Even after deductions, exemptions, write-offs, income deferrals, and whatever other accounting and legal arcana the rich throw at their tax returns, in the end, the typical one-percenter paid 32% of his income in 2018.

"It's clear that Americans have figured out the truth about who pays, because politicians are shifting the goalposts. Elizabeth Warren switched the conversation from what fraction of income the rich paid to what fraction of wealth they paid. President Biden has upped the ante by talking about taxing unrealized capital gains. This is unprecedented. The federal government has no constitutional authority to tax wealth, and never have unrealized gains been considered income – either in the realm of accounting or economics. An unrealized gain is simply an investment 'in process.' An investment's tale isn't told until the investor cashes out. Unrealized gains aren't gains. They are hypotheticals. What politicians want is to foment class warfare. If they can get the middle class and poor to resent the rich, those same politicians can expand the scope of federal taxation into areas it has never before touched.

"What's really going on is that politicians see a coming fiscal storm, and they are desperate to find new sources of revenue before it hits. Federal spending is out of control. Politicians know it and they know that they can't stop it. Those same politicians have realized that raising taxes isn't enough. They need new sources of tax revenue that haven't existed before. Their first step is to institute new taxes on wealth and unrealized capital gains. Once established, their next step will be to expand those taxes to the middle class. A day of reckoning is coming. Politicians hope that we'll keep pointing fingers at the rich so we don't notice who the real culprits are."

CHAPTER TEN
IMMIGRATION
TWO KINDS OF FREE

"Capitalism created the possibility of employment."
~Friedrich Hayek (1899-1992)

"The Constitution was definitely and specifically designed to hobble all people who are so foolish as to think themselves capable of leading others by compulsion. It so functions today to an extent exasperating to the authoritarians – which is why they want to get rid of it."
~Leonard E. Read

Our TV news carried a feature on a large crowd of local immigrants becoming citizens. Years ago, I went through the process of becoming a citizen. My mother was a Yankee from upstate New York, but she gave birth to me in Saskatoon, Saskatchewan. We moved to the U.S. when I was 9 years old. In order to join the Air Force when I got out of high school, I had to become a citizen. It was a simple process and about a dozen of us were naturalized that day.

None of the people in my group were going to get help from the government because there wasn't such a thing. Most of today's new citizens are poor and come from impoverished or war-torn countries. Upon arriving in America they get immediate financial help from the government. Unfortunately, this can become a way of life. As many as half of immigrants who are refugees will stay on welfare indefinitely. Of course many become hard workers and productive citizens. They will thrive and prosper in the land of opportunity. In Minnesota, we have a significant population of Hmong from Cambodia. They are educated and successful and quite proud of Sunisa Lee, the gold medal-winning gymnast.

The concern is that most of these new citizens will vote for leftists. They join the free stuff army, and they will vote for politicians who will keep the free stuff coming. They could be the deciding vote on socialized medicine and higher taxes. One exception would be people from Cuba or Venezuela who actually lived and suffered under socialism. Hopefully our new immigrants will come to see the benefits of capitalism and free markets and turn away from the Democratic Party. If not, our country will deteriorate as impossibly high taxes that fund endlessly-growing social programs sink our economy. Socialists will sacrifice our economic well-being for forced equality, political correctness and dictatorial regulations. In that case, say goodbye to the land of the free. A lot hinges on the political persuasion of our new immigrants. So far, it's not looking good.

Minority voters support the Democrats. That's why liberals so ardently support illegal immigration and even open borders. They disguise their sentiments as compassion, but in truth they want the votes so they can force their socialistic schemes on us. Illegal immigration at our southern border exists solely for that reason. The leftists believe the more the merrier. CNN's Anderson Cooper commented that "it's exciting that whites will no longer represent the nation's majority." It's only exciting if you're a socialist or a Marxist that spreads lies about the motives of white Americans. It certainly why these leftists want open borders. They are hell-bent on spreading their ruinous collectivist doctrines.

It was encouraging to hear that a few Hispanic voters in parts of Texas are starting to vote for conservatives. Most Latinos have sound values and are generally law-abiding. They embrace the conservative mantra of personal responsibility, two-parent households, delayed gratification and educational excellence. These Latino voters will have little sympathy with crime and misbehavior. Crime and looting will send them into the arms of the Republicans. Wouldn't that be transforming for America to have the Democrats' strategy of open borders backfire on them as Hispanic voters turned right?

For years my company shared our office building with the U.S. Immigration Service, with a steady flow of immigrants from Central America pouring into the building. At times, they crowded the lobby. For the most part they didn't speak English. I always smiled and tried to be friendly when I was in the lobby. One day, there was a young Central American Indian woman with five little kids. I said hello, but she looked unsure of herself and didn't reply.

I got to thinking about how she would fare in America without speaking the language. Would she be able to work? Who would take care of her kids? It was apparent she would likely have to be subsidized. The government would have to give her the money and services she needed. This is not unusual for immigrants. A former employee of mine had a job for years signing up Somali immigrants for various government payments. I have nothing against immigrants who are often hard working people. I would also not begrudge this woman with five kids the means to raise them properly. However, the U.S. is running nearly unmanageable debt levels because of the relentless growth in entitlements. Once you start these social programs, you can't stop them. They only grow larger. Ultimately they could prove to be terminal for the nation. The more subsidized immigrants we take in the closer we are to a day of reckoning.

One day, when I walked into the lobby, I spotted a little two-year-old kid with a cleft lip and cleft palate. I asked a man with him if he was the father. He barely spoke English, but I determined that the boy's mother was in the immigration office. Eventually I met the mother and with the help of an interpreter I suggested the boy have his cleft lip fixed. Of course, she had no money so I told her I would pay for it. Subsequently, I located a plastic surgeon in St. Paul who had worked on the Smile Train fixing these disfigurements. I called his office and arranged an appointment for the boy, and volunteered to pay for it. After a few weeks, a nurse called and told me the boy was scheduled for surgery. However she explained the boy was probably going to need two surgeries and it would be expensive. That alarmed me, but there was no backing out.

It was two years ago that the boy had the surgery and I have heard nothing further from the family, the hospital or the physician's office. Somebody had to pay for it, but it wasn't me. There must have been a government program that picked up the tab. That's fine with me. Frankly, I did not ask any questions.

A recent Los Angeles Times article blames the U.S. for the migrant crisis. Our financial support of Central American governments that fought left-wing insurgents led to the article's conclusion that the U.S. is the root cause of the crisis in Central America. In both North and South America indigenous people are primarily leftists. Peru just voted in a communist president. The killing of these leftists in El Salvador ostensibly backed by the U.S. leads the author to roundly condemn America.

Compare these supposed sins with the crimes of communist regimes. It's no wonder that successful people oppose them. 80 years ago this June, Russia made a hideous deal with the Nazis and occupied the Baltic states. In Lithuania, the land owners, professionals, and business people were shot or deported to Siberia. Some 280,000 innocent people rode in wagons to the gulags and few, if any, survived or returned. The agony and suffering of these good citizens dwarf anything you might blame the U.S. for. These crimes are just the tip of the iceberg for the communists that so many now want to run things.

Years ago, a client who bought gold from us explained how he escaped from Latvia. The Russians checked your hands. If they were soft, they shot you. He hid in the woods and rubbed his hands on the bark of trees until calluses formed. They were now the hands of a laborer and the Russians let these workers pass through the checkpoints. His father had hidden some $20 gold pieces in the wall of their house. He extracted the coins and used them to obtain passage on a cargo ship to Sweden.

I have an Asian granddaughter who graduated from high school this week. My son and his wife went to China seventeen years ago to get her. One of the nurses at the orphanage selected her for them to bring home and adopt. She turned out to be a wonderful, intelligent, poised and beautiful young lady. She graduated with honors and received an award from her class. Among the audience were families of the other graduates, representing several ethnicities. Asian, African and Hispanic kids both biological and adopted stood with their families. Everybody was all smiles and feelings of good will prevailed. It was the best graduation ceremony I've ever attended.

This is the America I know, not the one the left and the media promote. I have never heard any racist slurs or bigotry directed toward Asians that the left now claims to be so prevalent. I see no signs of this prejudice emanating from anyone I know or anyone I have ever known. The vast majority of Americans are not racist. They are accepting of all races who like them are striving for a good life. The radicals are trying to paint us as something they can sneer at and feel superior to. We can only continue to love and respect others as we of today's generations always have.

CHAPTER ELEVEN

MINNESOTA – STATE OF DENIAL

"Not only did the Democratic Party fail to object to the mayhem, but the city governments they controlled abetted, incited, and applauded the anarchy."

~James Howard Kunstler

A fter four months in Florida, my wife and I flew home to Minneapolis in time for a vicious blizzard that the TV weatherman called a bomb cyclone. Hopefully, this was the final round in what was the worst winter of the century. After a month of record cold, the left-wing Minneapolis newspaper finally stopped running articles promoting global warming. Couple the bad weather with our high state taxes and you have to wonder who is staying in Minnesota and who is leaving. Unfortunately we can no longer deduct state tax payments from our federal tax which gives us close to the highest federal income tax in the country. I'm constantly running into former Minnesotans who have become Florida residents. It's an epidemic.

We often hear the media referring to us as "Minnesota nice" as if we are nicer than people elsewhere. The Wall Street Journal made me laugh when they referred to our senator Amy Klobuchar as Minnesota "not-so-nice" for her abusive treatment of her employees. We also think we have a superior health care in Minnesota. However, outside of the Mayo Clinic, I have found Florida health care to be better.

The Florida population is now up to 21 million. Signs of growth are everywhere. They have no state tax, capital gains tax or estate tax. Minnesota's myopic liberals insist that a 48% tax rate will not be a factor in Minnesota's economic growth. In fact, a Democrat told my wife they like to pay high taxes to help with social problems. Another one told me how much they loved winter. We have wonderful summers and a hardy population of energetic people in Minnesota. However, the left is doing their best to drive them to warmer climates where the sticky fingers of government are less onerous.

Furthermore, crime in Minneapolis has gone ballistic with dozens of carjackings, armed stick-ups, purse-snatchings, shootings, assaults and burglaries. Fights among large groups of young men are reported in the downtown area and vandalism and graffiti damage property including the Vikings' football stadium. Some businesses have been robbed at gunpoint twice in one week. One driver had his car boxed in by several men who beat him and then took his vehicle. Another man was seriously injured when he tried to stop his car from being stolen with his wife and child inside. Women report being mugged and choked by thieves who steal their purses. Violence and shootings are engulfing the city with more than 500 carjackings by November of 2021. Somebody needs to get a handle on this and soon.

Author Paul J. Watson tells us, "Authorities in Minneapolis sent out a letter to residents telling them to prepare to be robbed and to obey criminals following a recent surge in robberies and carjackings. 'Be prepared to give up your cell phone and purse/wallet,' states the email, which also says that if a resident encounters a criminal they should 'do as they say.'"

Luis Farias, a business owner in Minnesota said, "Democrats were slow to condemn the violence in Minneapolis in May. Throughout a summer of riots and mayhem, Biden and his party had little to say as violent criminals rampaged through our cities. Those who want to live and raise families in safe urban communities will get no help from Democrats. In the weeks and months ahead, will you be safe inside your home if rioters come knocking? Will you, your family, and neighbors be able to go outside without the threat of harm? Do you trust criminals to police themselves? Any candidate who does not stand up against these destructive and destabilizing forces is an enemy of safe communities and law and order. Yes, some police reforms are needed. But we can't work toward them when violent protesters are allowed to terrorize innocent people and tear apart the fabric of our society."

Author David Horowitz tells us, "Minneapolis set the pattern repeated by Democrat authorities in all the major cities subjected to violent attacks, including Chicago, Philadelphia, New York, Portland, Atlanta,

Seattle, and Washington, D.C. The mayor and city council members in all these cities were sympathetic to the rioters and looters, and to their transparently empty claims of being 'peaceful protesters' for 'social justice.' Consequently, the authorities refused to deploy sufficient force to discourage the mobs, allowing them to own the streets. When local authorities did dispatch a token police force, they were so outnumbered that the criminal mobs turned on them, injuring thousands. Law enforcement on the run – or absent – was a green light to urban street gangs to conduct their own rampages and turf wars without fear of reprisal. The majority of the ravaged cities were run by Democrats, and had been for fifty to a hundred years.

"In Minneapolis, which was typical, the mayor, the city council members, the police chief, the attorney general, and even the officer who applied the knee to George Floyd's neck were Democrats. The police chief was also black. If there was a 'systemic' race problem to blame for what had happened to George Floyd in Minneapolis, Democrats were 100 percent responsible. And the same thing was true of every major city the Black Lives Matter mobs targeted. The posture of the Democrats was explicable only in terms of their racial ideology, which caused them to defend and applaud, as a protest for social justice, the movement responsible for the mayhem. To a man and woman, Democrat officials described the violent riots as 'peaceful protests.' Their vice-presidential candidate Kamala Harris called the mobs 'A Coalition of Conscience.' Six weeks after the Democrat establishment surrendered Minnesota to the insurrection, the property damages in that state alone had already reached $500 million."

Minneapolis is known as the city of lakes. We have a lake named Hiawatha after the poem by Longfellow and a lake named Nokomis after Hiawatha's grandmother. A stream called Minnehaha runs through the two lakes and over a waterfall that is a tourist attraction. Minnehaha supposedly means laughing waters, but in Longfellow's poem Minnehaha is Hiawatha's lover who comes to a tragic end.

The largest lake in the city was named Lake Calhoun, apparently after John C. Calhoun, a vice president who came from a slave state. Calhoun has been the name of the lake for 197 years dating back to 1820. John C. Calhoun first gained notoriety at age 28 by supporting the factions who defended the U.S. against British encroachment leading to the War of 1812. No doubt the lake was named after Calhoun for his patriotism in that period and not his later support of secession. Although he died in 1850, ten years before the Civil War, he is blamed for southern intransigence. No question he is a controversial figure in history and his views would find little favor today. Nevertheless, Calhoun is an important historical figure whose accomplishments should be considered in their historical context.

Nonetheless, the Minneapolis Park Board voted unanimously to change the name of the city's landmark lake from Calhoun to Bde Maka Ska. However, in the minds of most Minnesotans, Lake Calhoun will always be Lake Calhoun. It's hard to pronounce the new name. For those of us of conservative or libertarian bent, this new name is almost comical and further proof, if you need any, of liberal foolishness.

In Minneapolis, we have a large population of immigrants from Somalia. One neighborhood, known as Little Mogadishu, lies within a congressional district that elected the leftist Ilhan Omar. This harsh critic of America immigrated from a country notorious for its corruption, lack of security, armed conflicts and humanitarian crises. The Somalis often suffer from famines, malnutrition and starvation. Abuses against children and sexual violence against women and girls are commonplace. How fortunate are these Somalis who were able to leave this failed nation and come to America? Do they give thanks? Not too many. By electing Ilhan Omar, some of them reflect ingratitude.

Now comes Ilhan Omar's 18-year-old daughter to announce that she is a communist. Her Twitter bio shows a hammer and sickle. It used to be "liberal parents, radical children." Now its radical parents, communist children. Ilhan Omar's daughter, Isra Hirsi will attend Columbia this fall, a particularly good place to worship Chairman Mao and other murderous revolutionaries. Her stated goal is to eliminate capitalism.

In Cuba, where they have eliminated capitalism, they are still driving 75-year-old cars. To be a Marxist today you have to ignore a century of positive history, and growing prosperity worldwide. The countries in Africa, like Ethiopia, that have embraced capitalism are beginning to experience explosive economic growth. Countries like Somalia are becoming welfare states that are going nowhere. All of this is lost on Ilhan Omar who is more interested in depicting America as unjust. Her homeland would be a better place to look.

It must be a life-altering experience to be in a bar or restaurant when somebody starts shooting. Just the incredibly loud blast of a Glock pistol would be terrifying enough. In St. Paul, Minnesota recently, two bar patrons started a pistol duel that killed a young woman and wounded 14 others. This happened in an upscale area of the downtown populated by bars and restaurants. To say this is shocking is an understatement.

Unfortunately, St. Paul is in the process of embracing a more holistic approach to crime and punishment. Young felons are no longer to be incarcerated but counseled instead. Violent crimes won't keep youthful felons in jail but almost immediately will allow them to return to the streets. I'm no expert on the subject of criminal behavior, but this sounds like an impractical liberal experiment. I'm sure that those who are implementing this new policy mean well, but it's a hard sell when someone is gunned down in your city on a regular basis and violent crimes are increasing.

These frequent crimes may well turn the population against the "defund the police" movement and the soft-on-crime liberals. Nothing will turn a voter into a conservative faster than being a victim of a car-jacking or cowering in a restaurant while a gunfight goes on. Conservatives believe the way to combat crime is to put the criminals in jail. In light of the paralysis gripping the downtown areas of our cities, the voters may soon come to agree.

CHAPTER TWELVE

EDUCATION

"Higher education now stands for mob rule, civic ignorance and contempt for truth and free inquiry."

~John M. Ellis

"Government-provided free tuition tends more and more to produce a uniform conformist education, with college faculties ultimately dependent for their jobs on the government, and so developing an economic interest in professing and teaching a statist, pro-government, and socialist ideology."

~Henry Hazlitt

"Civilization can only revive when there shall come into being in a number of individuals a new tone of mind independent of the one prevalent among the crowd and in opposition to it. A new public opinion must be created privately and unobtrusively. The existing one is maintained by the press, by propaganda, by organization, and by financial influences which are at its disposal. The unnatural way of spreading ideas must be opposed by the natural ones, which goes from man to man and relies solely on the truth of the thoughts and the hearer's receptiveness of new truth."

~Albert Schweitzer

I once attended a social gathering at a fabulous home owned by an extremely wealthy Minnesota couple. They had inherited their wealth from their grandparents who had founded a highly successful business. Halfway through the party, the hostess gave several of us a tour of the home. Apparently, she and her husband slept in separate bedrooms because as we entered one room, she said this was her bedroom. Much to my amazement a large poster featuring Chairman Mao was fastened to the wall. I didn't say anything, but later I asked her brother, who was a staunch conservative, what's the story with the Mao poster? He told me she and her husband graduated from Columbia and they were both radicals. If anything, they should have been supporters of the free market blessings that capitalism had showed upon them. The brother blamed Columbia for his sister's communist persuasion. That was an eye opener for me.

Author Ben Shapiro explained what happened. "For decades, conservatives scoffed at the radicals on campus. They assumed that real life would beat the radicalism out of the college-age leftists. They thought the microaggression culture of the universities would be destroyed by the job market, that paying taxes would cure college graduates of their utopian redistributionism and that institutions would act as a check on the self-centered brattishness of college indoctrination victims. They were wrong. Instead, wokeism has been carried into every major area of American life via powerful cultural and government institutions – nearly all of which are composed disproportionately of people who graduated from college and learned the wokabulary."

John Ellis wrote, "One American institution – higher education – has decided to repurpose itself. It has set aside the job given to it by society and substituted a different one. Academia has decided that its primary purpose is the promotion of a radical political ideology, to which it gives the sunny label 'social justice.'

"Though most Americans aren't happy about this, academia has no qualms. No matter how many times the lack of intellectual diversity on politicized, one-party campuses is decried as unhealthy and educationally ruinous, the campuses won't listen. There was once internal debate about higher education's direction between traditional academic scholars and radical political activists, but that debate is long over. The activists, now firmly in control, have no interest in what the dwindling ranks of scholars have to say."

Author Jim DeMint writes, "America's college campuses are the intellectual headwaters of the 'woke' mob now poisoning the great rivers of freedom in our country. This mob has taken over the political left, devastated our cities and now threatens every American with traditional values and common-sense conservative views. Conservatives haven't taken radical professors, brainwashed students and cowardly university administrators seriously. The scholarship produced by woke academics in nonsense fields like anti-racism, critical gender theory, and ecofeminism never spilled out into broader political or cultural debates. Now we know that at least some of the children and adults steeped in the anti-American, anti-Christian, anti-truth narrative behind the 'Awokening' have launched a nationwide crime wave. If everything they've been taught is true – that America is racist and evil, that the Constitution is a weapon of oppression and that conservative speech is violent – then it was only a matter of time before some Chads and Emilys broke out the Molotov cocktails.

"These aren't just toddlers squabbling in a sandbox. The campus-led assault on free speech and equal justice – to say nothing of objective truth – are a clear and present danger to freedom, justice, and our constitutional order. And they are inspiring a rising generation of pseudo-fascists whose tantrums, however ignorant, are quickly amassing a frightening criminal rap sheet. Washington should cut these frauds and thugs off the federal gravy train, and make their access to taxpayer money contingent on them actually serving the taxpayers and the republic."

John Ellis continues, "Higher education now stands for mob rule, civic ignorance and contempt for truth and free inquiry. Far from being the leading edge of an advanced culture, the universities drag America back towards a more primitive state. They have contempt for the restraints and rules that define society, such as political neutrality and non-political institutions. For radicals, politics takes precedence over everything and every field within social science and humanities eventually degrades into a mere channel to spread progressive orthodoxies.

"In an advanced society, journalists have the vital job of keeping the citizens well-informed so that the government can be held to account. Only in less-developed cultures is the press commonly in firm political control, but since America's university journalism programs are now overwhelmingly left-activist, we effectively have the political press of an undeveloped nation. Same rules for school teachers, at present also trained by campus radicals, which is making public school systems increasingly ideological. Socialist dictatorships and banana republics hold their universities under strict political control; it's astonishing that the U.S. seems to be joining that club."

This is from Ammo.com: "Seemingly overnight, a large segment of

America has gone insane. It would have been fairly uncontroversial even five years ago to say that men should not be allowed to compete in women's sports, regardless of what they might subjectively 'identify as.' And yet, this is now a subject of contention across a number of sports, including mixed martial arts and powerlifting. What's more, having the wrong opinion and expressing it publicly might make you the subject of a public shaming, up to and including losing your job and being de facto blacklisted from your industry.

"Another, far more troubling development is how quickly a significant and powerful minority of Americans grew to believe that America is a fundamentally racist country and that white Americans are somehow uniquely evil by virtue of their birth. But this change did not come out of nowhere. In fact, it's the product of decades of indoctrination of generations of Americans through what is called 'education.' Since at least the 1960s, with significant acceleration in the 1980s, American youth have been indoctrinated with hostility toward Western civilization in general, with hostility toward whites, the nuclear family, Christianity, private property and men. Perhaps most troubling is the view that Western civilization is responsible for the lion's share – if not all – of the world's evil."

John Ellis writes, "Race relations in America are devolving under progressive leadership. Campuses are in a constant state of hysteria about 'systemic' racism, with small armies of diversity administrators always eager to jump at the slightest infraction, real or imagined. Why does invisible campus racism need such zealous policing? If radical leftists can persuade enough people that America is rotten at its core with racial prejudice, they'll gain traction for their program of radical social transformation. Power-hungry radicals whip up racial tensions where none exist because their authority depends on social division.

"In the past, universities were indispensable in maintaining American culture, but now they undermine and sicken it. The public should learn to see through the patina of prestige that still covers elite schools, and should assess realistically the damage these schools are doing today. That damage goes beyond a failure to develop graduates who think independently. Universities now attack the most basic principles of American society, and do so with lavish taxpayer support. We should decide how best to cut them off."

Author M. N. Gordon writes about the financial excess in higher education, "Without question, the student debt crisis is a disgrace. There are roughly 45 million student-loan borrowers who owe on the order of $1.6 trillion. The federal government is responsible for this mess. It supplied the credit that distorted the world in this way that would have otherwise been impossible. The massive amounts of federal student loans inflated a higher education bubble and an industry of entitled, fake intellectuals. Young adults have been told since before they could count that college was the magical path to a bright future. But as tuition costs ran higher, propelled by more and more student loans, the value proposition no longer penciled out.

"What would happen to all these high-paid professors and fancy country club style college campuses without all this government sponsored debt? For starters, tuition prices would fall. Professor salaries would also fall. And college campuses would adjust to their more modest means. Smaller budgets would help trim the fat, and eliminate many of the nonsense quack 'studies' courses. These courses have little redeeming value and only exist because they're funded by an abundance of federal student loans.

"The point is, $1.6 trillion in government-sponsored student loan debt has piled up. Forgiving this debt does not make it go away. Debt, remember, is unearned money that's borrowed from the future. It must either be repaid or defaulted on. Given that this is government-sponsored debt, the act of erasing it merely transfers it from student borrowers to the American public."

David Horowitz writes, "Today America is facing the most serious threat of the establishment of tyranny in its history. This threat comes from a political faction that calls its reactionary creed 'progressive.' Its goals are advanced under the Orwellian names 'Critical Race Theory' and 'Anti-Racism.' These doctrines have already been embraced by American universities and public schools, tax-exempt advocacy foundations, the corporate culture, and the Democratic Party. They are racist ideologies that indict every white person as a participant in an imaginary system of 'white supremacy' allegedly oppressing every 'person of color.' In this twisted perspective, any deviation from the political perspective of the Left – for example, on the need to maintain enforceable borders or to secure civil law and order, or to afford due process to the accused – is racist and potentially makes the person who holds that view a hate criminal worthy of suppression."

Mark Levin wrote, "Indeed, America's college and university facilities have turned their classrooms into breeding grounds for resistance, rebellion, and revolution against American society, as well as receptors for Marxist or Marxist-like indoctrination and propaganda. Academic freedom exists first and foremost for the militant professors, and the competition of ideas is mostly a quaint concept of what higher education used to be and should be. But Marxism is not about free speech and debate, it is about domination, repression, indoctrination, conformity and compliance. The existing society and culture and those who prosper within it (intellectually, spiritually, and economically), as well as those who defend it, must be denounced and defamed. Disillusion with the status quo is key. Marxism presents 'new faith,' if you will, which promises a new and better society, for which a passion if not obsession is inculcated in future generations – despite its trail of mass death, enslavement, and impoverishment. Brainwashing against the American founding and civil society, and indoctrination about activism and protest – even violent if necessary – are constantly preached throughout academia. The goal is to create a generation of revolutionaries."

CHAPTER THIRTEEN
ECONOMICS

"Leftists wrongly view the free market as a zero-sum game, in which some (the rich) gain only at the expense of others (the poor). In fact, the free market is a system of voluntary exchanges, and such exchanges take place only if all parties to them expect to benefit."

~David Gordon

"Under capitalism, everyone provides for their own needs by serving others."

~Ludwig von Mises

"Different people rise to the top under socialism than under capitalism. The higher the socialist hierarchy you look, the more you will find people who are too incompetent to do the job they are supposed to do."

~Hans-Hermann Hoppe

"Government can help the economy only by protecting you and your property. A free market economy, limited government, and the rule of law are the keys to prosperity and peace."

~Patrick Baron

The possibility always exists that a stock market decline, a jump in interest rates, or a weakening dollar can lead to something worse. The first reason to own silver is the potential for an unmanageable financial crisis. The second reason is hopefully to make a lot of money. For sure the most important reason is to get you through a financial catastrophe in one piece should it occur. An economic collapse can mean runaway inflation or asset deflation or both. It can mean an economic depression and financial collapse. Are these extreme events probable? Most people would laugh at such dire predictions. Nevertheless, these are real enough possibilities to make the ownership of silver sensible.

I have for many years studied the economic arguments of the Austrian school of economists. Their greatest thinker Ludwig von Mises would be issuing the most dire warnings were he alive today. Mises put it this way, "The boom can last only as long as the credit expansion progresses at an ever-accelerated pace. The boom comes to an end as soon as additional quantities of fiduciary media [money and credit] are no longer thrown upon the loan market. If the credit expansion is not stopped in time, the boom turns into the crack-up boom [hyper-inflation]; the flight into real values [hard assets] begins, and the whole monetary system founders. Continuous inflation [money and credit creation] must finally end in the complete breakdown of the currency system."

Frankly, there is no good way out. The monetary authorities will do anything to forestall deflation and a depression. Thus, they will destroy the purchasing power of the dollar. There is no middle road. Many people will be wiped out and only a few nimble investors will survive intact. David Stockman writes, "A poisonous brew of easy money, cheap debt, sweeping financialization and unbridled speculation has been injected into the American economy by the Fed and Washington politicians over the last three decades. It has turned Wall Street into a dangerous gambling casino while leaving Main Street buried under mountainous debts, faltering investment in growth and productivity and the hand-to-mouth economics of spending more than you earn. It has also left the American economy exceedingly vulnerable to external shocks.

"America's dangerous economic fragility stems in part from the fact that 80% of households have no appreciable rainy-day funds and businesses have piled their balance sheets sky high with debt and artificially extended their supply chains to the four corners of the earth in order to goose short-run profits and share prices.

"Shrunken household incomes and business cash flows are literally pulling the legs out from under the $82 trillion edifice of debt and speculation that has been piled atop the American economy. The 30-year party of false prosperity is over. And to boot, we now have a viciously partisan and progressive/woke government in Washington that has no clue about the impending fiscal and financial calamities."

In the rest of this chapter I've rounded up some of the best commentary on our current economic predicamen.

Economist Thorsten Polleit says, "Since the financial and economic crisis of 2008/2009, central banks have more than ever taken control of interest rates. They no longer limit themselves to setting short-term interest rates, but hope to control interest rates with longer maturities through purchasing government bonds, mortgage bonds, corporate bonds, and bank bonds. In this way, they directly influence bond prices and thus their yields. Market interest rates are no longer determined in a 'free market.'

"By controlling market interest rates, central banks have in fact put a 'safety net' under their economies and financial markets. As central banks have signaled to the public that they feel responsible for a healthy economy, and, in particular, for ensuring that 'financial market stability' prevails, investors can put two and two together. Should the economies or financial markets get to the verge of collapse, investors can expect central banks to step in, fighting the impending crisis. This understanding encourages investors to take additional risks, step up their investments, and disregard or underestimate risk.

"The central banks' safety net policies amount to a manipulation of the market system on the greatest scale possible. With basically all prices and all market yields distorted, consumers and firms inevitably get disoriented and make wrong decisions. However, under such conditions the boom can be kept going much longer compared to a scenario in which free market forces are allowed to do their job – that is, establishing financial asset prices as well as inflation, credit, and liquidity according to real-world realities. However, today's environment is rather different: central banks, in their attempt to prevent the current boom turning into another bust, have effectively corrupted the vital roles that financial markets and interest rates play in a free market system.

"Once the real trouble starts the boom turns to bust. Credit markets shut down, borrowers can no longer roll over their maturing debt, and no investor is willing to lend new funds. To prevent credit defaults and the collapse of the debt pyramid, central banks would presumably step in as 'lenders of last resort,' refinancing basically all kinds of borrowers in need. An outright inflation policy would begin. Nevertheless, capital consumption and economic regression would set in. People's living standards would nosedive; many would be thrown into outright misery."

M. N. Gordon writes, "The opportunity to face the economic depression honestly – through bankruptcies, write-downs, and a broad financial purge – came and went with the rollout of massive fiscal and monetary stimulus programs. Crackpot schemes now exist like the CARES Act, the PPP, the PMCCF, and the SMCCF, among others. The general objective of these programs is to replace the personal and business cash flows that the virus lockdown destroyed. The intentions may have been good, but they paved the road to hell. Efforts to paper over the drop in what people and businesses earn and what they owe, can't be covered for long. These programs were flawed from the start when they relied on printing-press money and credit conjured up from thin air to make them work. Printing-press money destroys the purchasing power of money that has been earned and saved. The consequences of mass money debasement are impossible to undo. Once printing-press money has mixed with the money that's been earned and saved, the value of all dollars becomes suspect.

"What comes next can be summed up with the word: 'More.' More monetary stimulus. More fiscal stimulus. More spending programs. More federal unemployment checks. More bailouts. More government-subsidized loans. More money supply. More Fed purchases of corporate bonds. More debts. More deficits. More of this. More of that. All of which will be paid for with more printing-press money."

Editor John Rubino writes, "The movements of long and short rates, both in absolute terms and in relationship to each other, tell businesses whether, where and how to allocate capital. Freeze the yield curve in place and the signal goes dark. Investors are left flying blind, with two results:

1. A lot less investment takes place because wise (that is to say risk-averse) capitalists recognize that they have no idea what

they're doing and choose to hoard their cash and refrain from borrowing more.

2. The deals that do get done feature a bigger percentage of mistakes – 'malinvestment' in economist-speak – which means the aggregate resulting cash flow is lower and the number of high-profile failures larger, resulting in a society that's both less rich and more unstable.

"Since this will be happening in a world where capital has already been misallocated on a vast scale (think share repurchases), increasing the outstanding amount of bad paper just takes us that much closer to the point of systemic failure."

CHAPTER FOURTEEN
CLIMATE AMBIVALENCE

"The Biden administration's plan to banish fossil fuels is a greater existential threat to Americans than climate change."
~Wall Street Journal

"In the United States, liberals have made it virtually impossible [to increase the supply of oil] by banning drilling in all sorts of places and preventing any new refinery from being built anywhere in the country in the last 30 years."
~Thomas Sowell

In reading about weather extremes reported daily in my city's liberal newspaper, it's hard to know what to believe about global warming. About the time the newspaper has me convinced that we are courting a climate disaster I read something like this from atmospheric physicist Richard Lindzen, "What historians will definitely wonder about in future centuries is how deeply-flawed logic, obscured by shrewd and unrelenting propaganda, actually enabled a coalition of powerful special interests to convince nearly everyone in the world that CO2 from human industry was a dangerous, planet-destroying toxin. It will be remembered as the greatest mass delusion in the history of the world – that CO2, the life of plants, was considered for a time to be a deadly poison."

Then the media continues to bombard me about the risks and dangers of climate change and I'm back on the fence. The fact that climate hysteria originates on the left makes me begin to doubt it for that reason alone. Progressives are wrong about almost everything and that may be the case with the green revolution. Author James Rickards gives us his two cents worth: "If you listen to the climate alarmists, they'll tell you we only have a few years to save the planet. If we don't eliminate CO2 emissions quickly, the planet will warm, sea levels will rise, storms will intensify, cities will be inundated, and lives will be lost to starvation, disease and dehydration. Every one of those claims is empirically false, but that doesn't stop the global power elite from trying to shut down the oil and gas industries and replace power generation with solar, wind and so-called renewable sources.

"The claims of the alarmists are worse than junk science. Solar and wind power cannot replace oil and gas in producing electricity to supply the grid. This is because solar and wind are unreliable. When the wind doesn't blow and the sun doesn't shine (which is often in most places), there is no power output at all. Solar and wind can supplement oil and gas (and nuclear power), but they cannot replace them due to unreliability and the expense of batteries. Get ready for higher energy costs, power outages, death and damage from cold spells, and possible lines at the gasoline pump. The Green New Deal is a policy fiasco in the making that will take us back to the 1970s."

Economist David Stockman follows with this broadside: "The climate hysterics is the greatest trumped-up crisis in modern history. The only thing less true is the assumption that a forced conversion of the U.S. economy to green energy will be an economic boon. Not to worry because a greenhouse gas purge will result in a huge increase in new investments for solar, wind, EVs, batteries, bio-fuels etc. and a cornucopia of jobs installing those investments and operating them thereafter. Nonsense!

"The very idea of s**t-canning our highly efficient stock of low-cost fossil fuel-based power plants, auto fleets, industrial facilities, aircraft, farm equipment, construction machinery etc. for high-cost green energy betrays profound economic ignorance. Windmills are not economically efficient, nor are solar panels in the vast areas of the country plagued by cloudy skies. And high cost battery storage of electrical power is far less efficient than natural gas-fired capacity when it comes to supplying power to the electrical grid during periods of maximum demand."

The economist and author Stephen Moore wrote a column recently in the Washington Examiner, and here are some excerpts: "Paul Ehrlich wrote one of the most famous and bestselling books of the 20th century. It was called *The Population Bomb*. It was 300 pages of doom and gloom. The planet was being destroyed because human beings were reproducing like Norwegian field mice. It was a Darwinian nightmare leading the species inexorably back to a Neanderthal subsistence-level existence. We learned this from the book's memorable and often-quoted, apocalyptic first sentence: 'The battle to feed all of humanity is over. In the 1970s and 1980s, hundreds of millions of people will starve to death in spite of any crash programs embarked upon now.' He predicted that highly populated countries such as India could not be saved from extinction. Overpopulation was to the 1960s, '70s, and '80s what climate change is today.

"Fifty years ago, we were warned of a coming ice age. The left is now frantically trying to erase that history and pretend that the global cooling warnings never happened. Now, these same scientists assure us we are facing a catastrophic warming of the planet. Well, which is it? It's 'climate change.' So, how did the green doomsday lobby get it so wrong? It turns out that mankind does not act like Norwegian field mice. We use our minds to reason. We respond to changes in the world around us. The left loves to look at short-term trends and erroneously extrapolate them out for 20, 50, and 100 years. They predicted that we would run out of food, oil, gas, farmland, drinking water, and clean air as Ehrlich did. Instead, thanks to human ingenuity and free markets, we have more food, more oil, more water, and clean air than ever before in the history of the planet."

Today's continuous climate uproar originates with the same liberals who fostered the environmental movement. According to author Robert Sheaffer, "'Environmentalism" is typically nothing more than a large-caliber weapon in the politics of resentment. It is merely a fig leaf to hide the ugliness of resentment against science, against technology, against economic growth (which always brings sinful profit to someone), and especially against civilization itself. 'Environmentalists' automatically oppose the construction of new roads, of major buildings and shopping centers, of airports, of mines, and most vehemently of all, of facilities for the production and distribution of energy – especially if they are nuclear. It does not matter whether the proposed development is ecologically and/or economically sound. All such developments are to be stopped wherever possible, using any suitable pretext whatever. If something cannot be stopped, it is to be delayed as long as possible in the hopes that future developments will be stifled by the exploding costs of interest on construction capital during the years of politically induced delay."

The conflicting arguments about the Green New Deal led me to order a book by Steven E. Koonin entitled *Unsettled*. The author is a Democrat and leader in U.S. science policy and carries a long list of credentials. The book jacket explains, "When it comes to climate change, the media, politicians, and other prominent voices have declared that 'the science is settled.' In reality, core questions – about the way climate is responding to our influence and what the impacts will be – remain largely unanswered. The climate is changing, but the why and how aren't as clear as you've probably been led to believe."

So, as I read this book I find out that it's not true that hurricanes and tornadoes are becoming fiercer and more frequent, nor are sea levels rising to any extent. The book advocates a slow approach to understanding climate science and disparages the idea that global warming will wreck the economy.

A book review by Mark Mills of the Manhattan Institute states, "As Mr. Koonin illustrates, tornado frequency and severity are also not trending up; nor are the number and severity of droughts. The extent of global fires has been trending significantly downward. The rate of sea-level rise has not accelerated. Global crop yields are rising, not falling. And while global atmospheric CO_2 levels are obviously higher now than two centuries ago, they're not at any record planetary high – they're at a low that has only been seen once before in the past 500 million years.

"Mr. Koonin laments the sloppiness of those using local weather 'events' to make claims about long-cycle planetary phenomena. He chastises not so much local news media as journalists with prestigious national media who should know better. This attribution error evokes one of Mr. Koonin's rare rebukes: 'Pointing to hurricanes as an example of the ravages of human-caused climate change is at best unconvincing, and at worst plainly dishonest.'

"When it comes to the vaunted computer models, Mr. Koonin is persuasively skeptical. It's a big problem, he says, when models can't retroactively 'predict' events that have already happened. And he notes that some of the 'tuning' done to models so that they work better amounts to 'cooking the books.' He should know, having written one of the first textbooks on using computers to model physics phenomena.

"Mr. Koonin's science credentials are impeccable – unlike, say, those of one well-known Swedish teenager to whom the media affords great attention on climate matters. He has been a professor of physics at Caltech and served as the top scientist in Barack Obama's Energy Department. The book is copiously referenced and relies on widely accepted government documents.

"But even if one remains unconvinced by his arguments, the right response is to debate the science. We'll see if that happens in a world in which politicians assert the science is settled and plan astronomical levels of spending to replace the nation's massive infrastructures with 'green' alternatives. Never have so many spent so much public money on the basis of claims that are so unsettled."

The radicals stumping for the Green New Deal are crazy enough to cast doubt on their extreme solutions. The Squad and their ilk want to eliminate the oil industry and spend unlimited amounts on unproven technologies. The government is already spending large sums on the construction of wind and solar power and subsidizing these developments with tax breaks. No one ever mentions the massive amounts of land all these non-intensive energy sources will require. Are we sure we want wind farms that will occupy – according to Princeton's Net-Zero Project – land areas equivalent to Arkansas, Iowa, Kansas, Missouri, Nebraska and Oklahoma?

Among the progressives, the rhetoric grows ever more heated and the charge of "climate denier" gives the leftists a feeling of superiority. They've been wrong before and they will be wrong again. In any case, the vast expenditures by our government on energy alternatives are just one more addition to our mind-boggling deficits. This comment from Bjorn Lomberg, a fellow at the Hoover Institution and author of

False Alarm; How Climate Change Panic Costs us Trillions, Hurts the Poor and Fails to Fix the Planet, offers the best advice, "Climate change deserves our attention, but policy makers need to be realistic."

CHAPTER FIFTEEN
FUTURE PAIN

"The more things a government undertakes to do, the fewer things it can do competently. When the government tries to do everything it must do everything badly. The essential function of the State is to maintain peace, justice, law, and order, and to protect the individual citizen against aggression, violence, theft, and fraud."

~Henry Hazlitt

"America is under assault from a variety of forces desperate to replace the America that launched on July 4, 1776. We have tolerated the forces of ignorance, radical ideology, and anti-Americanism long enough. It is time to reassert the rule of law, the spirit of America, and the potential of a genuine new birth of freedom. We must reject the rule of the mob and uphold government 'of the people, by the people, and for the people.'"

~Newt Gingrich

When my parents were born in 1910, they got to see horse-drawn wagons replaced by automobiles. They saw the first airplanes, movies, radio, television and computers. These advancements came about through the freedom and energy implicit in capitalism. Today, and throughout my lifetime, these amazing inventions, technologies, and breakthroughs continue. Advancements in medicines, transportation, electronics and entertainment seem endless. Only a nation of fools would tamper with this productive system. But that's what the left wants to do.

Our economic might, our entrepreneurship and our innovations are the one thing that can keep us out of terminal economic and financial crisis. Free markets can hold off the worst aspects of the gloom-and-doom scenario. We are going to have some hard times with inflation, deflation, recession and depression. Wealth will be reshuffled and many will suffer financial loss. However, as long as we don't let the government and the leftists destroy capitalism, we should be able to weather the storm.

However, I have this reoccurring fear that the present path of America is leading to something ugly. Emerson had it right when he claimed that too much success would lead to a great leveling. For example, the process of inflating can supercharge the economy and give us a temporary high, but inflation often accompanies the decline and fall of empires. Booms lead to busts. Hubris leads to pain and humiliation. Every indication points to the fact that we are in an era of excess. Is not free money for everyone excessive?

Massive government spending on welfare subsidies must eventually lead to a breaking point. Our government is passing out enormous quantities of money for every kind of human hardship or discomfort. Everywhere you turn, people are getting free money. Eventually this leads to the kind of inflation that erodes so much of the dollar's purchasing power that people don't want to hold it.

Now you have a situation where the welfare checks no longer buy much and the welfare recipients are angry. The government does everything in its power to pacify the unhappy citizens whose welfare payments, Social Security checks and government retirement checks are buying less and less. Huge dollar increases to fund the government's payments cause the inflation fires to burn out of control. Riots, demonstrations and civil unrest plague the nation. Law-breaking and violence are excused if it helps the needy. (Much of this is hypothetical, but some of it has happened in other countries that have experienced runaway inflation. However, no nation has ever had so many people totally dependent on government welfare payments.)

Rumors begin to circulate that the government is preparing a new currency to replace the sinking dollar. That's the final nail in the coffin for the dollar. Suddenly everyone rushes to spend their dollars and their value falls precipitously. Now the government checks buy little or nothing. The media and left-wing politicians are quick to blame capitalism and affluent citizens. A cry goes up to raise taxes to impossibly high levels. Radicals preach for the downfall of our system to be replaced by equal outcomes for all.

A new currency replaces the old dollar, but it is no longer the world's reserve currency. It buys little and a lengthy depression ensues for America. The excesses of the inflationary period are wrung out and the people must endure hard times that the government can't fix. Little patience exists for misbehavior and a strict application of the law becomes prevalent. In this dire period of pain and suffering, a new work ethic emerges and an improved respect for our nation's history evolves into hope and optimism. A bitter lesson has perhaps been learned.

Editor Clive Maund put his spin on the near term: "The normal business cycle where periods of growth were punctuated by healthy recessions has been all but eliminated by government and central bank interference. The recessionary phases which saw bear markets and retrenchment were essential for the maintenance of a healthy economy, because it involved the correction of excess and the elimination of companies that were inefficient.

"Politicians do not like the recessionary part of the business cycle, especially if it bites when they are the ones in office leading into an election, and so, if they can find a way to forestall it, they will. Before the gold standard was eliminated by Nixon in 1971 there was a limit to what they could do by pumping money to head off economic contractions. After 1971, they found themselves free to print more and more money and they could not resist the temptation to expand the money supply rather than exercise fiscal restraint. They found it much easier to expand debt in order to indulge in a "have now, pay later" ethos that has since become a universally accepted new normal. So started the parabolic debt curve that has been further fueled by derivatives that have allowed debt to ascend to astounding, giddying heights.

"Years ago, long before debts rose to their current crushing levels, it would have been possible to straighten things out and balance the books. It would have involved sacrifice and unpopularity and so was untenable with politicians, especially those in power. It was far easier to simply keep kicking the can down the road.

"The expanding debt and money creation has now gone vertical and resulted in such monstrous economic distortions that it has brought the global economy to the brink of collapse. There is now no way back

– things have gone way beyond the point of no return. The emergency measures introduced after the global financial crisis in 2008 that were supposed to be a temporary state of affairs, such as QE and zero interest rates, have now become permanent. They are accepted as a "new normal", but they are highly abnormal. Zero interest rates discourage saving, the basis of capital formation and instead encourage rampant speculation in often intrinsically worthless ventures. All the newly printed money is no longer stimulating the economy, so their response is to print more and more money. You can't generate real economic growth by simply pumping more money. All you wind up doing is destroying the currency and creating hyperinflation.

"The truth is Central Planners have gone all-in with their fiscal and monetary policies. In their zeal to keep the stock market in a perpetual bull market, they have borrowed and printed to the limit. Interest rates are now at or near zero throughout the developed world, and debt-to-GDP ratios have risen to the point where insolvency is now becoming a real risk.

"The future guarantees that the junk bond market will someday implode, and probably soon. Repo borrowing costs will soar, the liquidity in the junk bond market will evaporate and equity prices will begin to free-fall. However, since normalization has proved to be a pipe dream, as it has failed miserably whenever and wherever it has been even marginally attempted, policymakers are aware that they will be handcuffed during the next economic downturn. That is why central bankers have become petrified over each downtick in the stock market.

"The clock is ticking down towards a period of unprecedented economic tribulation, and its catalyst will be the implosion of the global bond bubble. A recession will destroy the worldwide corporate bond market. But even though that is bad enough, intractable inflation will destroy the entire global fixed income complex across the board. Modeling when this great reset will occur and capitalizing from it will make all the difference in the world for your standard of living."

From a political standpoint, should the radicals prevail America as we have known it will disappear. Down deep, these contemporary socialists are full of malevolence. Many are the same type of revolutionaries that put Castro and Maduro into power. A victorious left will abolish our Constitution, confiscate our assets, take away our means of defense and abrogate our rights. Nothing could be more serious than to have these collectivists triumph. We have prospered as a country because of the merit system, capitalism and free markets. Any change in this freedom formula will prove to be disastrous. Do not take these modern day Marxists lightly. They mean to do you in. The radical left has a history of recruiting and politicizing the criminal class to do their dirty work. Criminals make the best terrorists. Make no mistake about it, Marxists and Socialists want to destroy your way of life and they have plenty of support from the media and the useful idiots in the Democratic Party.

Author Christopher DeMuth advices, "Three characteristics that have endured from the founding are a live-and-let-live attitude, a belief in opportunity and initiative, and a strong sense of patriotism. The first two embody our ideals of liberty and equality; the third is the spirit that holds everything together.

"Today's woke progressives believe that these features of the American way are lies and illusions – to be 'woke' means to have woken up to the realities concealed by happy talk about liberty, equality, and opportunity. Progressives want to replace live-and-let-live with an identity politics of grievance and resentment among racial, sexual, and other groups and of envy of 'the rich.' They would replace equal opportunity with preferences and penalties for officially identified groups, and individual initiative with government provision for even routine incidents of life. By opening our borders, and by recasting our history as a story of unmitigated evil, progressives would depose American nationhood.

"A great many Americans remain attached to our traditional ideals and ways of life and are aghast at the strange ideologies sweeping their institutions, from Wall Street to local schools. But progressivism has become a powerful force. It draws upon the decline of family, religion, and locality and on the tribalism of social media and the internet. It has the advantages of passionate conviction, elite validation, and bureaucratic entrenchment. Which American way will eventually prevail is an open question."

CHAPTER SIXTEEN

SILVER

"Silver is well into a structural ongoing supply decline – made worse because most silver used in modern applications is not recoverable, and is thus lost for reuse. The trickle of additional new silver production coming online is simply not going to change any time soon."

~David Smith

Sometimes the greatest investment stories go unrecognized. For example, most investors never give a second thought to procuring a cache of silver coins and bars. This despite the claims of some experts that silver is a grossly undervalued asset. My company's silver consultant Theodore Butler, who writes a newsletter on silver, claims that silver is the profit opportunity of a lifetime. He suggests that silver could go up ten times or more.

Mr. Butler bases his opinion on a number of bullish factors that apply only to silver. He claims that the price of silver is set through futures trading on the COMEX. Weekly government reports from the Commodity Futures Trading Commission (CFTC) reveal that 4 to 8 large banks and brokers have sold short many millions of ounces of silver. This concentrated short position has held the price of silver to artificially low levels for years. This shorting has been extremely profitable for these big short sellers. Only in 2020 were the tables somewhat turned on the big shorts. Prices rose strongly for gold and silver and the short sellers were suddenly out $10 billion. If prices continue to rise, a possibility exists of a short squeeze that could propel the price of silver to much higher levels and crush the big shorts.

This vulnerable short position has attracted the attention of the recently famous short squeezers at Reddit/Wall Street Silver. The silver apes, as they call themselves (after the Silverback Gorilla), now number 120,000 and they have been buying large quantities of silver bars, coins and silver exchange traded funds. Their goal is to drive the price of silver up to the point where the big eight short sellers must buy back the silver they have sold short in order to stem their losses. That would put the price of silver into the stratosphere. Mr. Butler, the world's foremost silver expert, claims that being short silver today is dangerous beyond measure. He points to numerous additional reasons silver is poised to dramatically break out to the upside.

First of all, silver is an industrial metal and a superior conductor of electricity. It's used in virtually everything that requires electricity such as cell phones and computers. It also has growing use in solar panels. Silver fits the requirements of green energy along with dozens of other industrial applications. Mr. Butler goes on to explain that silver is the only commodity with a dual demand profile. In other words, it has investment demand on top of industrial demand. Even a small increase in investment demand can bring on a shortage. Butler further believes that an inevitable shortage will cause the industrial users to hoard and stockpile silver no matter what the cost. They must have silver or go out of business. This will push the price up even further.

A large contingent of buyers purchase silver primarily as a hedge against inflation and economic crisis. Any further worsening of inflation would likely lead to even more aggressive accumulations of silver coins and bars by investors. During much of 2021, delays in filling orders and shortages led to premiums on coins over their bullion value.

Historically, for thousands of years the ratio of the gold price to the silver price was 16 to 1. This important ratio is now much higher. Some argue that this ratio must be restored based on the growing demand for physical silver. More importantly, the price suppression of silver on the futures market for so many years has led to greater usage by industry of this cheap commodity. Nobody has bothered to find a cheaper substitute. At the same time, the low price has discouraged construction of new silver mines and mined-out silver deposits have not been replaced. Nearly two-thirds of silver mine production comes as a byproduct of copper, lead and zinc mining so the production of silver cannot be easily ramped up.

The commodity futures market regulator, the CFTC, has been paying more attention to the precious metals market lately. They have worked with the Justice Department to charge silver traders at JPMorgan,

HSBC, ScotiaMacotta and Deutsche Bank for illegal trading practices. Most were charged with spoofing, a market ploy where large sell orders are placed to drive down the price and then withdrawn before they are executed. Consequently, if the CFTC moves to force the end of the large manipulative short positions, that would also set the price of silver free. As with any investment, there are no guarantees that silver will skyrocket as Mr. Butler believes. Nevertheless, he has articulated a powerful argument that silver should be bought and held.

Twenty-one years ago a friend told me about Theodore Butler who supposedly knew a lot about the silver market. I decided to call him and was quickly impressed with his knowledge of gold and silver. When Mr. Butler talked about the potential price gains ahead in silver I began to see an opportunity for both my company and our clients. Mr. Butler was a former commodity broker with Merrill Lynch and he had a completely different analysis of the market than what I'd been used to. My company looked at silver in terms of supply and demand. We saw prices impacted by the dollar, interest rates, inflation and deflation. Ted Butler argued those factors were mostly meaningless in determining the price of silver. He claimed the price was set by futures market trading on the COMEX. He named a number of big banks that dominated and manipulated this futures trading.

The thing that got my attention was his insistence that a few big banks were controlling prices through short sales. They had figured out a way to harvest big profits through market manipulation. The silver price was artificially depressed through these antics. Therein lay the opportunity for investors. Once the free market price was reestablished, it would be at much higher levels. Ted Butler wrote a few articles for our newsletter explaining his theories. It was so convincing I structured a deal with him to be an independent consultant exclusively for Investment Rarities.

Silver was under $4.00 an ounce when he predicted it would rise ten times. In the years that followed, it did exactly that. Subsequently, he pointed out JPMorgan as the chief manipulator and short seller of silver. Recently he's shown that banking giant JPMorgan has abandoned their short sale manipulation and accumulated a vast hoard of physical silver at low prices they engineered. (Four of JPMorgan's silver traders have been indicted for spoofing, furthermore, putting in fake sell orders and then withdrawing them.) Thus silver has lost one of the big factors that has depressed the price. The main thing that Mr. Butler has always stressed is that artificially holding down the price of silver caused an increased demand and a reduced supply. That long term distortion will be resolved by silver reaching its free market price which Mr. Butler insists is much higher. He also suggested that the manipulation has made a silver shortage inevitable. This, he claims, will lead to prices so high they will be written about for a hundred years. Nobody knows more about silver than Mr. Butler. He is a pioneering thinker and probably the most plagiarized analyst in the history of the precious metals market. We are lucky to have him.

Another commodity analyst, Richard Mills writes, "Industrial demand for silver is projected to notch an 8-year high of 524Moz in 2021. It seems clear to us that the role of silver is changing. Once referred to as 'poor man's gold' for its affordability or 'the devil's metal' for its volatility, silver has been given a new makeover as a green metal. The most conductive of all the metals, silver is ideal for use in solar panels, 5G, and automotive applications including EVs which use up to twice as much silver as regular vehicles. The need for silver in all three applications is going up. Silver demand for 'printed and flexible electronics' is forecast to increase 54% over the next 9 years. According to Sprott Insights, silver plays a critical role in all 'green revolution' discussions, even more fundamental than cobalt, lithium and nickel, battery metals that are more usually associated with electrification.

"The United States, Canada and other countries that have committed to lowering carbon emissions are going to need more silver, to go into electric vehicles, charging stations, 5G, and for the cables connecting new wind turbines and solar farms to the grid. Supply is limited. We have already reached peak mined silver. Silver mines currently do not produce enough silver to meet demand without recycling. It's the same situation with gold and copper.

"For now, as long as prices remain where they are, the industry will be able to melt down enough silver to meet demand. But this isn't a sustainable model. Because silver is more of an industrial metal than a monetary metal, there is a limited amount of above-ground silver available for recycling. Eventually the industry will reach a point where they have to either get more production from existing mines or find new silver deposits. The latter can't be done in a hurry; it takes seven to 10 years at minimum to build a mine and often longer.

"For the three areas of growing demand – solar, 5G and automotive – where is this new silver supply going to come from? According to Sprott Insights, 'We do not see enough supply growth to offset the demand growth,' with mine supply falling since 2016 and 'we do not see enough projects in development to generate the kind of production levels in question, at least not at current silver prices... Our view is that the 'green revolution' will be highly positive for silver.' It's hard to disagree with that, and the obvious conclusion is that silver prices are heading higher."

The fact a few large banks have used unsavory tactics to hold the price of this important mineral down has created some powerfully bullish consequences. The historically low price has discouraged mining for silver. Many discoveries have been made that have never been mined because of the low level of profitability. Furthermore, prospecting, drilling and exploring for silver deposits has diminished greatly. A lot less silver has been mined and consequently much less exists above ground. In fact, so little currently exists that a surge of investment buying on top of the existing industrial demand would likely lead to a shortage.

A silver shortage would most certainly lead to a price explosion. That, in turn, would lead to a buying panic among industrial users who must have silver or go out of business. Thousands of companies rely on silver. The low price also nullifies any significant search for alternatives to silver. As the price rises, industrial users won't have anything cheaper to switch into.

Silver deposits are primarily epithermal, which means they are generally deposited near the earth's surface. The big deposits like Leadville, Cerro Rico de Potosi and the Comstock Lode were on the surface and easily discovered. Most of those big deposits are mined out. Mining companies now have to do more costly deep drilling. Consequently, discoveries tend to be smaller. Almost two-thirds of the silver mined now comes as a byproduct of copper, lead, zinc and gold mining. That means the production of silver is price-insensitive. In other words, no matter how high the price of silver, mining companies won't increase their production of these other metals to get more silver.

All these factors will eventually be understood and the silver market will change forever. We've always had periods where investors have poured into silver. Inevitably this has caused the price to go through the roof. We are patiently waiting for this event to happen again. When it does, the world's foremost silver analyst Ted Butler claims that the gains will be huge. We can't begin to comprehend the small amount of silver available in comparison to the enormous amount of buying power that can be directed into it. According to Mr. Butler, the price rise to come will be written about for centuries.

Author Jeff Clark advises, "The growing green revolution requires the use of silver. Due to its unique chemical makeup, silver is one of the elements that make green technologies what they are. Silver is used in most electrical generation today because it has the highest known electrical and thermal conductivity of all the metals. And when it comes to green electricity, solar is one of the fastest growing segments of the market. Solar is green because it is a renewable energy source and emits no carbon emissions. The amount of silver used in solar panels can vary, but a fair average is about 20 grams, or 0.643 troy ounce, roughly two-thirds of an ounce. We put 23 solar panels on our roof earlier this year, so we used 14.8 ounces of silver. That may sound like a small number of ounces but it adds up quickly.

"In California, a new law will require solar on every new building of four stories or less. Other states and countries could easily follow suit. And by any measure, the use of solar in our society is poised to grow significantly. Solar costs less and can be installed faster than most other energy sources. This makes it especially appealing to second and third world countries. Both China and India are on track to see a significant increase in solar capacity. It's not just solar but all renewables. Windmills use silver too. Brushes that contain silver are used in the motors and generators of wind turbines.

"Electric cars and trucks require more and more silver. This category includes electric vehicles, battery electric vehicles and plug-in hybrids. These vehicles use more silver than the internal combustion engine. The electric engine, battery pack, and battery management systems all require silver. While the amount of silver used in a Tesla and other electric vehicles is small, the aggregate total adds up quickly – and will only go higher.

"It's not just electric vehicles, either. Autos in general are becoming more 'electrified' every year. The majority of electrical connections in a car use silver-coated contacts – silver switches are used to start the engine, control electric seats, and open/close electric windows. Silver is also used in heated seats, window defoggers, and luminescent displays. This all means that silver demand for this sector is set to rise at a fast clip."

I started a company called Midwest Silver Distributors in the early 1970s when silver was under $2.00 an ounce. I would cold-call successful businessmen and try to get an appointment with them to explain the potential of silver. One of my first sales was to my mom and dad. They bought three bags of 90% silver coins for $1,200 each. The face value of a bag was $1,000 so their maximum risk was $200 a bag. By 1980, silver had risen twenty-five times. My dad called me on the day silver hit $49 and asked if they should sell. That thought was farthest from my mind because we were all sure that silver was going to $100 an ounce.

My parents could get over $100,000 for their silver and that was a lot of money at the time. It would be enough to maintain their modest lifestyle for the rest of their lives. I called my dad the next morning and told him to bring the silver to my office and we would buy it. We were buying huge quantities of silver coins, silverware and gold jewelry at the time. Thinking about my parents selling influenced me and I sold my silver too. By 1980, Investment Rarities had over 100 employees and most were mad and disgusted when they heard I had sold my silver.

Unfortunately, I didn't have the good sense to tell our clients to sell their silver. It was just too radical at the time. So the question remains, when is it time to sell? Some people argue that if something goes up ten times (a 10-bagger) it should be sold. On the other hand, a newsletter I read suggests never selling your silver coins and bars and passing them on to your heirs. I'll probably follow that advice because the economic future is so cloudy.

One thing you should not do is sell too soon. We have clients selling back to us every week because they have patiently held silver for many years and are tired of waiting. However, it's good to remember there isn't much silver available and investment demand is accelerating. I also suspect that industrial demand could be greater than we are told because of its use in billions of cell phones and millions of automobiles, to say nothing of computers, electronic devices and solar energy.

The goal with silver is to make a large profit rather than a small one. When you consider the vast increases in newly created money to offset the economic contraction, the future gives cause for concern. Holding on to silver should give you comfort.

Finally, what do you do with your money if you sell? There may not be better options. Interest rates are low so bonds and savings can be diminished by inflation. Stocks are risky. Real estate requires expertise as do art and antiques. The more you ponder what to do with your money the more uncertain the answer. For me, until silver rises to much higher levels, it's a great asset to hold. At some point in the future we can revisit the question of when to sell.

In the 1970s I wrote a lot about inflation. I thought I was pretty smart because I predicted double-digit increases in the cost of living and that's what happened. In the early 1980s, I kept beating the drum for inflation, but it never happened. I was wrong and our business suffered. It was humbling, embarrassing and stressful. I was warning people about things that never happened. Since then, I've been reluctant to make sweeping economic forecasts. I harkened to economist John Maynard Keynes' comment, "There's a lot of ruin in a nation." In other words it takes a long time for financial ruin to unfold, if it ever happens. If we are going to have a crash, it seems like it will be a slow motion crash. In fact, we are slow-walking toward serious consequences all the time. I don't know how and when the crisis will hit, but I do know that creating trillions to pay the bills won't work forever. We are monetizing our debt and that has been the death of many a regime. This suggests that the dollar and other currencies will continue to lose purchasing power as they have for decades.

To offset this damage you should own and hold tangible assets. The most liquid tangible assets are gold and silver. We recommend you purchase the following silver bars. The silver kilo bar struck by the Swiss Pamp Refinery in Switzerland is 32.15 ounces of .999 pure silver. These attractive bars have a serial number and a certificate from the mint. The Pamp logo is stamped into the bar with the .999 purity of the bar. A Mint box contains 15 bars.

We also recommend smaller silver bars. They come in 5- and 10-ounce sizes that are portable, attractive and highly reflective. These bars are .999 pure silver. They are struck by private mints with the utmost precision and care. These bars are supremely liquid and prized as items of high intrinsic value everywhere in the world. They stack nicely in a home safe and they are impervious to damage by the elements. Their glistening surface and beauty explain their popularity.

The 100-ounce silver bars produced by the Royal Canadian Mint are the nicest 100-ounce bars ever minted. They are long, flat, bright and shiny. Each one is approximately 8.333 troy pounds of .9999 pure silver. The polished surface of the bar is stamped 999.9 between two small maple leaves. There is a serial number and the words FINE SILVER, the French ARGENT PUR, and 100 oz t. A large, round Royal Canadian Mint logo with a modernistic maple leaf is featured on the bar.

For large amounts of silver we have storage available at Brink's for 1,000 ounce silver bars. The storage agreement is exclusively in your name and carries the serial number of your bars. There's no commingling or other dubious practices at Brink's. We also have safe storage available at our bank in suburban Minneapolis for 100-ounce bars. When you want to sell, you sign a release for the bank, we pick it up and send you a check.

Prior to 1965, U.S. coinage was made of 90% silver. Today these coins are found in $1,000 face value bags. A bag contains 10,000 Roosevelt dimes, 4,000 Washington quarters, or 2,000 Kennedy or Franklin half dollars. You can buy them in uncirculated condition or in circulated condition. The bag of uncirculated coins has 725 ounces of silver and the circulated coins have 715 ounces of silver. The uncirculated coins come in rolls and they are bright and shiny. The circulated coins have minor circulation wear, but still look excellent. You can buy a full bag, a ½-bag, a ¼-bag or a 1/10-bag. These coins would be of great utility in a period of runaway inflation as a means of exchange.

Another popular type of silver coinage are the one-ounce silver coins struck by mints in Canada, Austria and the U.S. These coins are .999 pure silver. Canada produces the silver Maple Leaf, Austria the Philharmonic and the U.S. Mint the Silver Eagle. These coins come in rolls of 20 (25 for the Maple Leaf) and are traded the world over.

You may want to own silver in your IRA. We use GoldStar Trust as our primary custodian. You can transfer from your present custodian to GoldStar. We give you the paperwork or you can download it from GoldStar. Once your account is established and funded, we complete the transaction. The assets go into GoldStar's account at the Delaware Depository. For more information on silver, please call us at 1-800-328-1860.

JAMES R. COOK *is the president of Investment Rarities Incorporated in Minneapolis, a company he founded in 1973. Mr. Cook is the author of a best-selling book, The Start-up Entrepreneur, and the novel Full Faith and Credit.*
Mr. Cook has received the National Wetlands Conservation Award from the U.S. Fish and Wildlife Service, for preserving and restoring wetlands. He is also the architect of the website neverforget.net, a new way of looking at the horrors of the Holocaust.

INDEX